Rave Reviews coming in . . .

Layne Dicker Reviews "For the Love Of Greys"

Well known and respected Avian Behaviorist, author and lecturer Layne David Dicker offers the following observations after reading For the Love of Greys:

Nothing would be easier than to make sweeping and superlative comments about Bobbi Brinker's "For the Love of Greys." It is, in fact, wonderful and should be required reading for anyone interested in breeding or keeping not only grey parrots, but all parrots. However, the book is best flattered by its contents. Bobbi has researched the most current information available on diet and nutrition and gives practical advice regarding feeding. Bobbi has taken the basic training of "Up" and "Down" to the next level. Common misunderstandings about greys and baths, dietary calcium, breeding protocol and biting behaviors are explained clearly and logically. A list of what this book contains could go on and on. But the most telling part of this book is the fact that, mixed in with top-notch information and an unsurpassed understanding of African greys, is an essential respect for and humanity towards these wonderful birds. Bobbi's feelings about the need to support research and conservation, and to treat any relationship that you might have with a parrot as a treasured privilege shine through every page. The information alone would make this book essential; the "message" will make it timeless.

Reviews are coming in from other publications as well and all agree that For the Love of Greys is a "must own" book for African Grey owners. Following are excerpts from those reviews.

Parrots Magazine . . . Reviewer Tracy Gwillim says, "The first thought that struck me when beginning to read this book was that here is a lady who is most definitely in love with African Greys - it shines through every page. . . . "If anyone is considering embarking on breeding and hand-rearing Greys, the chapters on breeding, handrearing methods and weaning should be required reading by law as it clearly shows the dedication needed to do it properly! I Thoroughly recommend this book, both to novices looking for their first baby and also seasoned Grey owners, as it cer-

tainly describes the commitment needed when sharing our lives with these delightful parrots." *(you can read the entire review in the August/September 99 issue of Parrot's Magazine)*

The AFA Watchbird . . .Carolyn Swicegood reviewed For The Love Of Greys and had this to say: "The information about African Grey Parrots shared by the author goes well beyond simple description. She offers clear and relevant direction regarding all aspects of care and breeding of African Grey Parrots. Her love and respect for these birds is obvious throughout the book. . . . "Although the title, *For the Love of Greys,* leads one to conclude that this book is exclusively about African Greys, it is sure to become an important guide and reference for owners of all parrot species. I highly recommend this "must own" book for the novice and expert alike." *(Carolyn's complete review appears in the November/December issue of The AFA Watchbird magazine)*

Exotic DVM . . . For The Love Of Greys was reviewed in the Exotic DVM Veterinary Magazine Volume 1.6 by Gwen Flinchum, DVM. Dr. Flinchum wrote, "Numerous books have been written on African greys, most of which contain general technical information. *For the Love of Greys,* however, is based largely on the experiences of the author, who is a long-time African grey breeder. As a result, this book gives much insight into what shapes the personality and thus pet quality of African Greys. . . "This book should be on the reading list of anyone interested in these birds, and it is a must for prospective African grey owners"

SCA Magazine . . .The Society for Conservation in Aviculture Magazine also reviewed "For the Love of Greys." Following are excerpts of that review: "There is so much information crammed into this book; I feel all Grey owners would find it invaluable for long-term reference. There are years of experience shared with the readers." . . . "The chapters on breeding, handrearing methods and weaning should be required reading... thoroughly recommend this book . . ."

The Real Macaw . . .Following are excerpts from a review by Beth Shery Sisk, member of The Real Macaw Parrot Club. . . "For the Love of Greys" by Bobbi Brinker, is the best guide you will ever use if you have, or are planning to bring, an African Grey parrot into your home. The book's 29 sections take the reader through the bird's life cycle, from an egg through adulthood. While a good portion of the information could be applied to all parrot species, Greys, in particular, have special needs and the author addresses them directly. Based on her vast experience with this special bird breed, the author's passion and respect for Greys is evident throughout the book's 130 pages. *(Beth's complete review appears in the June, 2001 issue of The Real Macaw Newsletter)*

Original Flying Machine . . .Reviewer Elizabeth Gurklys comments: *"For The Love of Greys"* by Bobbi Brinker is a must-read book for all African Grey owners. It is packed with lots of lovingly delivered information about behavior, care, feeding, breeding, weaning, and raising greys. When reading this book, it is obvious that Bobbi has a long-term special relationship with greys. Not owning a grey, I thought this book would give me some more information about these fascinating birds, I got more than I expected! Not only did I learn about greys, but the information contained in this volume can be applied to many other species.

For the Love of Greys

The Complete Guide
to a Healthy and Happy African Grey

Bobbi Brinker

Lucky Press

ISBN: 0-9760576-1-1

Published by:
Lucky Press, LLC
126 South Maple Street
Lancaster, Ohio 43130
U.S.A.

Publisher's Contact Information:
Phone: 740-689-2950
Fax: 740-689-2951
E-mail: books@luckypress.com
Website: www.luckypress.com

Disclaimer: The information contained within *For the Love of Greys* is based on the author's considerable personal experience with African grey parrots. This advice is not intended as a substitute for the medical opinion of an avian veterinarian, and parrot owners are well-advised to consult with an avian vet on medical matters. Neither the author nor the publisher will be held responsible for any loss or damages as a result of the reader following the information contained within this book.

About the Author . . . .

Bobbi Brinker's passion for the intelligent and elegant African Grey led her to 15 years of offering well-socialized, well-weaned Grey babies. Her fascination with, and understanding of, the African Grey evolved into a theory of management techniques designed to improve the lives and increase the understanding of this most special companion bird.

Her lifelong belief that education is the key to the successful management of any undertaking led to the establishment of seventeen bird mailing lists. The Grey Connection, established in 1997, is one of the largest bird email lists on the Internet. The Bird911 list disseminates reports of lost, found, and stolen birds across the Internet to facilitate the reunion of these birds with their owners.

Many of the articles in this book have been translated into Italian, Japanese, Russian, and Polish on the World Wide Web. Many of her articles have been reprinted in bird club newsletters, nationally and internationally and offered as educational handouts at conferences and bird fairs.

This book and her articles are given by other breeders to their clients to help them better understand and manage their African Greys.

Bobbi's articles have appeared in *Bird Talk* magazine, *Exotic DVM Veterinary Magazine,* and *The Original Flying Machine* magazine.

Acknowledgments

I owe an enormous debt of gratitude to the hundreds of African Greys I have known over the years. Their experience in captivity has led me inexorably to my conclusions and concepts of their management.

The creation of this book would have been impossible without the assistance and support of Susan Friedman Ph.D. and Marcella Remund.

Susan is a professor in the Psychology Department at Utah State University. Her areas of specialty are emotional disturbance in adolescence and applied research in human behavior. She was uniquely qualified to lead me to understand and accept my untutored application of facilitation and behavioral momentum to our beloved Grey birds. These concepts naturally foster non-controlling, non-punishing, gentle, loving ways of interacting with and teaching Grey birds.

Marcella is a doctoral student in English Literature/Creative Writing at the University of South Dakota. She taught English courses at the University of South Dakota for six years—Composition, Literature, Honor's English, Business Writing, and Creative Writing courses. Her real claim to fame, on both on the Internet bird lists and elsewhere, is as Captain of the Grammar Police.

Elizabeth Campbell, whose artwork graces the title page of this book, is a self-taught artist with work in collections all over the world.

Elaine Boxdorfer, with her 30 years of experience in printing, typesetting, and publishing, was untiring in her efforts on my behalf.

Carol Highfill, owner and creator of Birds N Ways, gave me the world by publishing my articles in *Winged Wisdom.* For this, I will be forever grateful.

I deeply appreciate the guidance, creativity, and hard work of Janice Phelps, Editor in Chief at Lucky Press, who made this edition of my book a reality.

Table of Contents

Living With Greys: Imposing Less, Facilitating More

Greys are intrinsically gentle creatures who manage their affairs without aggression. They are attentive birds who give themselves in a cautious manner. In our hands, Greys either reach their potential as intelligent, devoted companions, or they become distressed and difficult, or withdrawn.

It is true that, in part, a well-behaved Grey is one who has been taught how to adapt to living well with humans. Perhaps less well considered, and infinitely more important, is that a well-behaved bird is one who is kept by a human that knows how to adapt himself to living well with a bird.

The fact of the matter is that humans, unlike Greys, do tend to manage their affairs aggressively—defined in Webster's New World Dictionary as, "...a bold and energetic pursuit of one's ends...in a favorable sense, enterprise, initiative." In the pursuit of a pet bird who never bites or plucks, always stays put, welcomes strangers, and adores showers, we are often too bold, too energetic, and too punishment oriented. Where Greys are concerned, it is possible to be too aggressive in our attempts to change them, fix them, make them, and break them.

To a Grey, aggression portends death. They don't have the mindset or the tools to deal with aggressive behavior from humans. To wild caught, abused, or neglected birds we are nothing less then menacing, overpowering giants; how terrifying we must be to them. It will take many, many, many more years of effort, understanding, and patience to undo the lessons these birds have learned about humankind.

Our handfed babies haven't known the threatening side of humanity and it is essential that they never do. Continued reassurance, gentleness, and a tender, soft touch are the ways to a bird's heart. This begins with your breeder but most of the responsibility for a secure and well-behaved bird is in your hands.

Grey birds respond eagerly to facilitation and not at all to domination. Facilitation refers to a teaching style that eases your bird into the positive behaviors necessary for living with humans. If the goal is a well adjusted, loving pet, there will be little success with power strategies. Forcing birds to do what they don't want to may result in the desired behavior but it will not produce the relationship with your birds you so hoped to have when you acquired them.

It is mutually beneficial to birds and their humans to adapt to one another. This realization will not elude your bird. Like children, Greys have long memories and their personalities are deeply influenced by their experiences. Each and every interaction between a bird and a human is a lesson that teaches something to the bird about people. Each lesson either builds or diminishes trust. Thus, you must arrange all your interactions to be peaceful, respectful, patient, and understanding. Trust is the basis for all successful relationships between Grey birds and their humans. To build a lifelong relationship based on trust, begin by imposing yourself less and facilitating more.

"Up" And "Down"

A good place to start building a trusting relationship with your Grey bird is to teach him to step Up and Down when asked to do so. Up and Down are easy behaviors to teach a young bird and once mastered, they are tangible displays of communication and mutual respect. A reliable Up/Down response can be also used to facilitate compliance with other requests.

The handfeeder can start teaching Up/Down with very small Grey babies by saying "Up" each time a baby is picked up and "Down" each time he is put down. The baby won't be able to comply because he is still too little and weak, but he will soon learn that when he hears "Up", he will be picked up and when he hears "Down", he will be put down. It is reassuring to the babies to know what is going to happen to them. Reassurance is an important element in facilitating confidence in a Grey.

As the bird gets older and stronger, "Up" can be accompanied by picking up the two front toes on each foot, balancing the bird's weight on your hand, and gently lifting

straight up, while repeating "Up". "Down" should be used when the bird is placed on the floor or a low perch in the weaning and regular cages. Each foot can be placed on the perch using "Down" several times. It is important not to let go of one foot until the other foot is securely on the perch.

If your bird hasn't been trained from an early age, you can teach the Up/Down response by gently pressing your first two fingers into his lower abdomen, while repeating "Up". As the bird shifts his weight toward you, slowly roll your hand towards you as he grasps your fingers. If he doesn't step up, gently grasp his toes in the manner described above for babies. To teach the Down response, place the bird's tail behind the perch and say "Down". Always take care to wait for him to fully position one foot before allowing him to step backward off of your hand with the other foot. Some birds prefer to step forward. You can put your hand under and behind the perch so that it is in front of your bird as he steps down.

Whenever your bird complies with your request, enthusiastically and lavishly praise him. He has made a choice to respond to you out of love and respect. It is a gift. After all, when you are born with a hydraulic vise in the middle of your face or are willing to die of starvation rather than eat a new food, you really don't have to do anything you don't choose to, do you?

The Underlying Process

There is an important underlying process when a person makes a request like "Up" and a bird responds eagerly and willingly. By stepping "Up", the bird is demonstrating that he understands what you want and that he wants to give it to you. The bird has made a choice to move toward you, not against or away from you. This is a very positive process that affirms communication and promotes a trusting relationship.

There are two benefits to teaching your bird to respond reflexively to the Up/Down prompt: First, your bird will always have something he can do to please you, something he can do right. This is a powerful strategy for relationship building. No bird needs to be sent to the proverbial "dog house", no interaction needs to be left unsuccessful when a well-timed "Up" results in immediate compliance. This, in turn, will have a definite calming effect on a frustrated person as well.

Second, with a well-developed Up/Down response, you will have an effective tool to redirect any negative behavior your bird may exhibit into a positive interaction. Whatever the misbehavior, a cheerful "Up" request triggers a positive chain of events: The bird complies and you smile, praise, and kiss lavishly. You and your bird are now "facing the right direction" and can continue to interact positively from there. This is called behavioral momentum. You break the negative momentum with a request that the bird can do easily and automatically; thereby facilitating a new momentum, positive momentum.

This perspective is very different from the popular "flock leader" theory in which the Up/Down response is used to assert dominance over your bird. I truly believe this notion has no place in the raising of Grey birds. With either approach, facilitating or dominating, your bird will likely learn the Up/Down response. However, when the former approach is used it offers a requesting, respectful, appreciative tone—in other words, it sets the stage for relationship building. With the latter approach, the tone is commanding, challenging, and insistent. These are very negative, adversarial tones

that are picked up by the bird and are likely to make him fearful and suspicious. The desired short-term outcome is the same —the bird steps up—but one way fosters a relationship between you and your bird, the other way threatens to diminish it.

For whatever reason, fear, previous history, or a rebellious stage, some birds choose not to step up when requested to come out of their cage. This is a good opportunity to guide your bird into compliance. Remember that each and every interaction you share with your baby teaches him something about you that either hastens or delays your relationship with him. In this situation, you can give the bird a choice to step up on your hand or to come out wrapped in a towel instead. Be sure to remove the bird gently and consider what your attitude conveys. Removing the bird from the cage in a towel must be done regretfully, calmly, and without aggression. Try to convey that although coming out is not negotiable, the manner in which he comes out is up to him and that in either case, you will be gentle and kind. Your attitude is very important. When you bring your bird out in a towel aggressively, impatiently, or with a "now you're gonna get it" frame of mind, you will give the bird more reason to be afraid and bite you.

With patient persistence and without punishment, your bird will soon choose to respond to your Up request to avoid the towel. You will have found a gentle way for your bird to decide to do what you want him to do. Even if it takes a while, the important thing when facilitating behavior is that the bird chooses how to behave from a thoughtfully arranged set of choices. Negativity, force, and punishment are not only unnecessary but will work against your relationship in the long run.

Eventually, "Up" and "Down" will become so automatic that the bird will lift his foot at your approach or when you extend your hand to him without even hearing the word "Up". And, he will step down onto the perch when placed near it. Your Grey bird will use his intelligence and love to obey your authority as caretaker and decision-maker because it is the sensible and fulfilling thing to do. He has experienced only devoted care and kindness in the past and he trusts that this will continue in the future.

When A Grey Bites

Learned biting provides another example for facilitative teaching. If a bird is prevented from developing the biting habit, he won't bite without a reason. Once that is established, the reasons or circumstances that prompt a bird to bite can usually be avoided. I have a bird that bites me hard if I pick up the phone while holding him. I don't know why he does this so I simply avoid his bite by putting him down before I pick up the phone. What could possibly be gained by imposing myself on this bird and insisting that he not bite me while I hold him when I am on the phone?

Another strategy to avoid biting is distraction. With close observation you will soon learn the body language of an impending bite. Keep small foot toys nearby and offer one to the bird if it looks like he is going to bite. Craft clothes pins, a ball point pen cap, Gerber baby toys all make good foot toys that are equally satisfying to the beak as human skin. You can also rely on the Up/Down response to interrupt and redirect an imminent bite.

If avoidance and distraction don't work, the interaction between you and your bird should be calmly but perfunctorily ended. Return your bird to his cage or play gym.

The attitude you want to convey is indifference not anger. Discontinuing the interaction when it is not pleasing to you is a natural consequence of the bird's choice to bite. It is not a punishment. Here you are relying on the strength of the relationship you are working so diligently to develop with your bird. If all is as it should be, he will not want to discontinue interactions with you and will choose to stop biting. Consistency is an important element in facilitating non-biting birds. You must respond to biting the exact same way with each and every instance: Terminate the interaction swiftly but with indifference. A bird will learn quickly not to bite if he wants to continue to interact with his beloved person.

Of course, your bird must view you as his beloved human for this strategy to be effective. If you are not viewed so, what difference would it make to be removed from you? That means that all punishment tactics must stop in order for a loving relationship to grow. When a Grey bites, do not strike his beak or other parts of his body, do not drop him to the floor or "earthquake" him, do not isolate him in a cupboard or bathroom, do not cover or lock him in his cage. These behaviors are aggressive. Your bird will counter your aggression with escalated biting, confusion, and fear, or he will simply make no connection between his behavior and yours.

Finger Biting

Don't allow your bird to play with your fingers in his beak. If young birds are allowed to amuse themselves by chewing on you they may not accept petting without chasing your fingers or nibbling your nails. This behavior too easily becomes a finger nipping habit that is more difficult to stop than it is to avoid in the first place.

Even when the bird is just exploring, gently remove your finger from his beak and distract him. Put him on your knee, pet him as you usually do, and offer a foot toy when he goes for your fingers. Don't jerk your hands or fingers away, just remove them from his beak range and divert him with the toy. Your knee is also a good location from which to prevent your bird from nibbling buttons, zippers, clothing, or jewelry. If distraction doesn't work, simply replace your bird on his cage or perch indifferently, as described above.

Common Reasons For Biting

Some birds will attempt to bite when they are being returned to their cages. If the bird doesn't have enough out of cage time, biting is an understandable reaction. If the bird is allowed out for only a short time in a 24-hour period, he may be feeling contentious. This could lead to biting because he doesn't want to be put into his cage for another extended period of time. If out-of-cage time is increased to a minimum of four hours each day, he will likely be ready to return to his cage without biting.

Birds sometimes bite when their feet or toes are pinned, that is, when their toes are pressed securely against your hand or fingers with your thumb. Those birds that can't tolerate this should simply not have their feet pinned. Avoid head-on confrontations with your bird.

Adult Family Members

A well-behaved bird should at least tolerate adult family members other than his favorite person. Never force a bird to go to someone that he is unwilling to go to. One training method appeals to the stomach. If the less favored person in the household is the only one who gives a bird his most favorite treat, the bird will, in his own best interest, allow a relationship to develop with the person who holds the treat strings.

To encourage relationships with family members or friends try Sally Blanchard's game: First, instruct each person in the correct way to hold the bird. Be sure he is held in a way that is familiar and comfortable. Any interaction between Greys and children should be supervised. Next, sit in a circle on the floor and pass the bird from one to another taking a moment to speak softly and reassuringly to him. A bird who is hesitant to go to others but does so when requested by his favorite person is doing you a big favor. Praise him for his courage and trust in your judgment.

Roaming

A clumsy, slow moving bird that is comfortable on the floor is in grave danger of being stepped on, harmed by other companion animals, or harming himself with electric cords and other threats in the environment. Fortunately, teaching a bird to stay put is another behavior that is responsive to gentle facilitation. No matter how often they leave their approved location, simply replace them there again; and again; and again. Keep your attitude matter-of-fact. Do not allow yourself to get frustrated but do not relent. This is an opportunity that will teach your bird more than where to perch. Your bird will learn that you are serious about his care and your commitment to kindness. It is just the kind of interaction that cements your relationship with your bird and often results in a new level of respect. Eventually, he will give up roaming as a waste of time and energy. No negativity, the bird decides.

It is important to our babies to know their home range territory but this should not be accomplished by letting them roam at will. Instead, take the bird to all the rooms of the house. This will accustom him to the concept that places exist even though they are out of sight and it can reduce the anxiety of the unknown and the unexplored. A basket or tabletop t-stand can be taken along for the bird to sit on to keep him safe.

Shoulder Sitting

Most Greys can safely be allowed on your shoulder using the word "ok" or some other cue. Using a cue consistently will teach him that you decide when he is permitted on your shoulder. A bird must have a reliable "Up" response before allowing him to sit on your shoulder. He should have mastered the concept that nothing of you or on you is available for nibbling including your face, ears, jewelry, and clothing. Shoulder sitting is a privilege for well-behaved birds. If your bird refuses to step up immediately when requested or nibbles, calmly remove him from your shoulder and place him on your knee. Here you will be able to control him when he tries to run up your arm to your shoulder. You don't even have to say "No". As with roaming, be patient and resolute. Soon your bird will choose to behave appropriately to get access to the close interaction sitting on your shoulder provides. He will learn that he is allowed on your shoulder with the "ok" cue and can stay there as long as he follows the rules.

Maturity - Your Bird's And Your Own

The result of gentle, non-punishing teaching strategies is a bold, confident, curious bird who adores his person or family and is polite to the rest of us. The mature bird feels in control of the predictable environment that we have succeeded in establish-

ing for him. Control, predictability, choices are all important to facilitating a well-adjusted Grey bird.

One of the ways a mature bird expresses control over his life is by deciding stubbornly when and from whom he solicits petting. One of the saddest things about your baby bird growing up is losing the unqualified mushiness of a baby bird. Now, it is your turn to respect the decision-maker. Do not force yourself on your mature bird. With all you have taught, learned, and shared you have a different close and intimate relationship with your bird. Allow him this choice. Enjoy his invitations when he offers them.

Conclusion

People are usually quick to love and trust their birds. One look at that puddle of ink flopped out in his brooder and we are goners. It's a wonderful human trait but one that is not always shared by our birds. Raising a well-behaved companion bird is a commitment to a life-long role of teacher, supervisor, and patient guide. Too often people wonder why, at the ripe old age of six months, their bird still roams or is hesitant to come out of his cage. They feel discouraged and disappointed. It is your job to generalize the gentle techniques discussed above in new ways and to new situations to facilitate well-adapted behavior in your Grey. But we must always remember: Your Grey bird is a wild creature whose inward-directed eye and instincts are at war with his dependence on us. Above all else, his struggle must be viewed with kindness, compassion, and patience. His willingness to give kisses on demand and lower his head for your human touch is not owed to us; rather, his willingness is an extraordinary gift to be treasured.

The African Grey Myths

So many myths surround this sensitive and intelligent companion bird. Some of these myths have assumed the status of fact by virtue of repetition, but repetition does not make them true. Some of the most common myths are "Greys are clumsy", "Greys need more calcium", "Greys pluck", "Greys are one person birds". Nothing could be further from the truth.

Myth I - African Greys Are Clumsy

Greys in the wild are graceful birds. Gracefulness is an innate characteristic of Greys and it does not disappear in our domestically bred birds. When one finds a "clumsy" Grey, I believe that the bird has been made so by his human caretakers. Clipping a baby Grey's wings before he has learned to fly is the major human act that fuels the myth of the clumsy Grey. A bird's graceful potential is profoundly affected when he has not been permitted to learn to fly.

Learning to fly with proficiency and a systematic bountiful weaning program are two of the most important intervals in a bird's life. A Grey baby who is allowed to develop his flying skills benefits from it for the rest of his life. While learning to fly, a Grey learns valuable lessons in coordination and control. The awkward clumsy Grey of myth is a bird who has been denied his birthright by his human caretakers.

Self-confidence, elegance, and coordination result when a Grey is allowed to develop flight proficiency as nature intended. Fear, insecurity, and clumsiness adversely affect a young bird and can produce an adult who lacks the sense of self required to live in harmony with humans. Self-assurance and a belief in one's abilities benefit a bird as much as it does a human.

A second major cause for a Grey being clumsy is clipping a bird's wings incorrectly. A severe or improper clip, even though the bird has learned to fly, can contribute to loss of confidence. A bird's inability to control his body can cause fear and insecurity. If too many feathers are clipped, a bird will have no lift and can fall to the floor and injure himself. The long strong flight feathers provide lift and power. It is this lift and power that must be controlled through proper clipping. The goal is to provide safety indoors and to help prevent escape. The line is a fine one and custom clipping the bird is the key to achieving these goals. The shorter secondaries provide control and should never be clipped. Poor clips can result in clumsy landings, the inability to corner, and loss of balance and control while attempting to fly or flutter to the floor. Detailed information on why and how to clip Greys is described in Wingclipping and the African Grey.

Improper toenail clips may also contribute to a perception of clumsiness in Greys. Greys' feet appear to be too small for their weight and body configuration. When one considers the foot size of similar weight birds, it is apparent that Greys have smaller feet and more slender toes. A too-short toenail clip hampers their natural sure-footedness, balance and perching. Greys should have slightly longer toenails than other species. To determine if the toenail is the proper length, place the bird on a flat surface. The tip of the toenail should rest on the flat sur-

URLs for articles listed can be found under "Recommended Reading" in this publication.

face without lifting the pad on the bottom of the toe away from the surface.

Follow these simple guidelines and you will have a graceful, confident, and secure bird.

Myth II - Greys Are Pluckers

Plucking seems to occur more often in Greys because they must be managed more carefully than other species. Internal conflicts involving environment, cage, diet, activities, bathing, discipline, training, amusement produce internal disharmony and anxiety. The companion Grey may internalize these events and be unable to resolve them in a non-destructive manner. When something is amiss, they may express their discomfort or anxiety by feather plucking.

Plucking such as illustrated above is not normal behavior in African Grey Parrots. The beautifully feathered bird on the right is a well adjusted companion for his owner.

Greys need to be helped, more than other species, in developing their sense of self and self-confidence. They need to be encouraged to explore and to express their curiosity. They need to be exposed to change, movement, color, and variety and to learn that these are not things to be feared. A good breeder will get a bird off to a good start. It is up to the new owner to continue to expose the bird to variety and change.

While much plucking is behavioral, a medical cause must first be ruled out. So a trip to an avian vet is the first step in the process. Please see <u>Diplomates of the American Board</u> <u>of Veterinary Practitioners, Certified in</u> <u>Avian Practice November 1998</u>. While board certification provides no guarantee, it may reassure the owner that the vet has experience and knowledge of birds. Collaring or drugs in the absence of skin mutilation should be the last option—not the first.

Physiological feather chewing or plucking may be caused by: kernel peanuts, seeds or nuts (in the shell) contaminated with mycotoxins, low blood calcium, some bacterial/viral/fungal infections, allergic-type reaction to preservatives or artificial colors, heavy metal poisoning, internal or external parasites, and dry itchy skin associated with molting or infrequent baths.

Some psychological reasons may be: decreased interaction with the bird's preferred person, decreased

out-of-cage-time, lack of interesting or new or chewable toys, a too small cage, isolation, stress, lack of sleep, and insecurity.

• If the cause could be a psychological one, change the environment or location of the cage to a more protected spot, increase out-of-cage time and bird/human interaction, buy new toys (no rope or cloth toys), put the bird in a busier part of the house (the place where you spend the most time) but place the cage against a wall or in a corner for a feeling of security. Position the cage where the bird has a longer range view of those who enter his living area. Avoid a location where there is a lot of traffic back and forth past the cage. The sudden appearance of family members, guests, or other companion animals can contribute to uneasiness and insecurity.

• Reduce stress from the presence of other companion animals, children, pressure to socialize with a disliked person, arguments/shouting/loud voices, or household commotion.

• Provide a widely varied soft food diet that is comprised of birdie bread, beans/grains mix, sprouts, fresh fruits, and veggies. Choose fruits and veggies high in Vitamin A for their immune system benefits. A plucking bird is usually a stressed bird and he may need the immune system boost that high Vitamin A foods provide.

• Often seeds are implicated in plucking. Some birds can have an allergic-type reaction to some components of seeds or the seeds may be contaminated with mycotoxins. If the plucking is of recent onset, the seeds may be contaminated. Discard the seeds you are presently feeding and buy fresh clean seeds. If there are peanuts in the mix, discard them.

• Peanuts are often a culprit. They may be contaminated with mycotoxins and other bacterial or fungal organisms. Remove all kernel peanuts from the diet. Remove all nuts in the shell from the diet. Mycotoxins again are of concern. Hard-shelled nuts appear to be impermeable but how often have you opened a nut to find fungal growth or spoilage? I don't recommend that birds be fed kernel peanuts or dry seeds or nuts in

the shell. Offering Planter's type nuts from the supermarket may be safer if you choose not to remove nuts from your bird's diet. Do not offer Brazil nuts—these and peanuts are "notorious sources of aflatoxins". Ref. Avian Medicine pages 536 and 1043. For information on fungal organisms, a listing of articles is included at the end of this section.

• Consider changing the bird's diet from seeds to pellets. Chose pellets without chemical preservatives and without artificial coloring. If, however, the bird prefers or will only eat a pellet that contains chemical preservatives or coloring agents, this is a better, safer, and more nutritious diet than a seed diet. Once a bird is switched to pellets, the introduction and acceptance of a non-color and preservative-free pellet is easily accomplished using the same methods as the original switch to a pellet diet. The diet of a plucking bird must undergo careful scrutiny, as Greys are often adversely affected by an unsuitable diet. Please see Switching Your Bird To Pellets.

• If you are presently feeding pellets to a plucking bird, switch to a pellet without chemical preservatives or artificial colors. It is possible that the bird may be reacting to the preservatives or the colors. Some birds, like some humans, may be sensitive to preservatives or dyes. Many bird food providers will send free pellet samples. The bird may like one brand better than another. Hagen's Tropican, Harrison's Bird, and Zeigler Feed are some of the brands that don't contain chemical preservatives or artificial colors.

• Has the plucking bird been screened for zinc or lead poisoning? The zinc in quick links (and toy components) has been implicated in some plucking—so has paint from the cage and flecks from the base metal. Replace the quick links with stainless steel ones, check for peeling paint, and other possible sources of zinc. Remove all access to any item containing lead. Refer to <u>Poisonous Foods, Metals & Compounds</u> for information about lead poisoning. Marine supply stores, some bird toy manufacturers, and hardware stores are a good source for stainless steel quick links. An article that addresses zinc poisoning is <u>The A - Zinc of Zinc Poisoning</u>.

• Some success has been reported using aloe and water for spray bathing. Aloe Vera gel or juice is safe and nontoxic. It has excellent anti-itch and anti-burn properties and may provide relief if itching is present. Use only the gel or the juice, as Aloe Vera cream is oily.

From Carolyn Swicegood: "The sooner treatment is begun, the better the chances of cessation of this frustrating problem, as the long-term habitual plucker is more difficult to treat. Try filling a spray bottle with four parts pure water and one part Aloe Vera. (Do not use cold spray on the bare skin of a feather-plucked bird). It can be made stronger or weaker as needed."

• Drenching daily baths help hydrate the skin and feathers. It is especially important to bathe a bird daily during molting. The emergence of new feathers may cause itching and discomfort. If the bird starts to pluck during a molt, it may become a habit.

• Added humidity may be helpful. Our homes are a desert environment for our tropical birds. Heating our homes in the winter dries out the air and air conditioning in the summer removes moisture from the air.

• Add a product such as Citricidal to the water in the humidifier to avoid exposing the bird to airborne mold or fungal spores. Citricidal is a safe and non-toxic additive to water for disinfecting and control of unwanted organisms. Please see: <u>NutriBiotic</u>

<u>and Citricidal, The Criticidal Story</u>, and <u>The Kitchen Physician VII - Citricidal: Cure & Disinfectant</u>.

• Boredom or lack of attention may be another cause of feather plucking. Has time out of the cage or bird/human interaction decreased? If that is the case, it is important to increase interaction (minimum 45 minutes daily of direct and shared attention) and out-of-cage time (minimum 3 hours per day). Ref. Layne Dicker <u>Time Well Spent With Parrots</u>.

• Provide some new and interesting complex toys and activities. Roll up a TV Guide and stuff it in the cage bars. Wrap up treats and hand toys in newspaper or brown wrapping paper and put them in a basket or small cardboard box on the floor of the cage. This can provide hours of entertainment.

• Placing chunks of food on skewers can be a time consuming and interesting way for the bird to forage. A bunch of carrots with the top attached or a head of celery can keep a bird occupied for a long time. The addition of safe branches in the cage for chewing and stripping may help.

• Shred milk cartons as toys for birds to preen. Filling the bottom of the cage with balls of newspaper to tear up may be a substitute for plucking or feather shredding. Knotted leather laces may also be offered but the laces must be very thick ones to avoid entanglement. Plucking birds need "jobs" and hours of busy time while confined in the cage.

• Regressing a plucker to a happier time by feeding hot wet foods by hand may be comforting and reassuring to the anxious bird.

• Some birds may pluck because they aren't getting enough sleep. Providing a small sleep cage in a quiet part of the house for 10 or so hours of uninterrupted sleep may help.

• An improper wing clip is often the cause of a bird starting to pluck.

• It is best to watch everything that is done to your birds—no matter by whom. Improper handling by a vet/groomer/stranger or a traumatic experience with them can have an adverse effect on a bird. This source of anxiety, fear, and stress may cause the bird to become a plucker. Don't let anyone take your bird into another room without you for a procedure.

• Children or other companion animals may torment some birds in the absence of the primary caregiver. Eliminate unsupervised access.

Since the finite cause of plucking is very difficult to determine, these suggestions may or may not decrease or halt the plucking. The more quickly plucking is addressed, the better chance there is of stopping the behavior before it becomes a habit. A consultation with an experienced sympathetic avian behaviorist may address the behavioral aspect of plucking.

Articles on feather mutilation:

Feather Mutilation

The Complexities of Feather Destructive Behavior

Quaker Mutilation Syndrome (QMS)

How to Manage Feather Picking

Using Homeopathics.... Psychological Feather Picking

Feather Picking in Pet Birds

Articles on Aspergillosis:

Aspergillosis Part 1

Aspergillosis Part 2

Infectious Diseases of Birds

Aspergillosis

Summary of Avian Diseases

Aspergillosis

Myth III - African Greys Are One Person Birds

Greys are flock animals. A Grey in the wild has relationships on many levels— parental, sibling, juvenile flock acquaintances, older and wiser flock members, bonded mate, and parent to chicks among others. Communicating and interacting with many other birds is natural behavior for Greys.

To restrict the number of relationships and the humans a Grey interacts with and is civil to is contrary to his inborn propensities. Greys need their flock; and in captivity, humans must satisfy this need. Greys may take time to develop relationships, but these relationships are very necessary for their psychological well being.

Those who wish to have a relationship with a Grey must earn the privilege. Greys appear to be more cautious. I believe one of the reasons is because they are part-time ground feeders. A bird on the ground is more vulnerable than one who feeds in the treetops. When one is vulnerable, it pays to be careful and cautious. This caution spills over into other aspects of a Grey's life. A Grey's sensitivity to nuance and the environment, coupled with his caution and careful assessment, are a challenge we must meet if the Grey is to realize his full potential as a companion bird.

The favored person has to be willing to share the bird for the bird's own good and has to be willing to persuade the bird to be civil to others. He/she should not be afraid that others, family or wife or husband, will "steal" the bird's affections.

Developing relationships with multiple people also depends on those who wish to have a relationship with the bird. A Grey's love and trust have to be earned. They are not given to those with whom the bird has only a peripheral contact. If other family members aren't willing to make time for the bird, then the bird will not love, trust, or be willing to interact with them.

A Grey should not be coerced into relationships with family members who are not willing to make the effort or take the time to establish their own relationship with the bird.

If there is no one in the family who is interested in the bird except the owner, the bird may become a one-person bird by default. If at all possible, the owner should expose the bird to friends, neighbors, and knowledgeable bird keepers.

While it may be flattering for the favored person to have a bird who is unwilling to be touched by others, it is not good for the bird to have his world so narrow and confined. While we think that our life circumstances will not change, this may not always be the case. A civil well-behaved Grey will always have a home and loved ones should the unthinkable occur—divorce, death, separation, etc. The more relationships and the wider the circle of acquaintances a Grey has, the healthier it is, emotionally and psychologically, for the bird. Thought must always be given to the fact that a Grey can have a human life span and may have more than one home in his long life. How much better for the bird if he is gentle, well behaved, and accustomed to the attentions of others. Such a bird will never be passed from home to home—his pet potential decreasing with each move.

Gentle, kind, and patient handling will ensure that your bird is a pleasant, well-behaved, lifetime companion. Cast yourself in a parental role. Be a teacher, a mentor, a model, a guide rather than an authoritarian figure. For our companion birds to love and trust us, we must be considerate and gentle with them. A calm kind-hearted approach will pay dividends that last the bird's whole lifetime.

Coercing "good" or "acceptable" behavior from a Grey will place a heavy stress load on this sensitive being. A Grey cannot be punished into "good" behavior. He will turn his anger and frustration at this dominance inward. Coercion never brings love and trust; at best it brings grudging compliance. The price of this compliance may be illness because of the stress on the immune system, acting-out because of the frustration, and avoidance, distaste, and distrust of the dominating one. Often this distrust is reflected by a general dislike of humans. Attempting to dominate a Grey is a recipe for disaster—for the bird and for the owner.

The development of a Grey's personality is on-going. As in humans, the past, the present and the inevitably changing environment all contribute to the dynamic development of personality. The humans in a bird's environment have an obligation to understand and accept that the bird has a right to be himself. Consistent, kind and patient handling and management of this ever-developing and maturing bird is the key to a happy bird and a happy owner.

Myth IV - African Greys Need More Calcium

Of all the myths, this one dies the hardest death. Greys need enough calcium, like other birds. They do not need more.

Calcium plays a role in blood coagulation, maintains normal heart rhythm, transmits nerve impulses, calcifies egg shells, contracts the uterus during egg laying, and activates several enzyme systems. Seizures, as well as leg paralysis, have been associated with low blood calcium. Sudden collapse or fainting is characteristic of advanced calcium deficiency in Greys. Of all the species, Greys are most likely to suffer seizures from low blood calcium.

Anecdotal stories suggest some feather plucking may be caused by inadequate blood calcium levels.

Excessive levels of blood calcium can cause very serious and life threatening renal problems—mineralization of the kidneys and the renal tubes.

Be very careful with calcium supplements. Indiscriminate and excessive use of these supplements is dangerous and could become life threatening. The only time a calcium supplement should be given to a companion bird is after an abnormally low blood level is diagnosed and an avian vet prescribes supplementation.

The best way to prevent problems is to have a blood calcium level test done at the annual exam and to take your bird to the vet immediately at the first sign of illness. Since birds hide symptoms of illness, by the time there are symptoms (of whatever disease process), they are very sick indeed.

If a Grey is on a pellet-based varied diet, and such a diet may include high calcium foods such as almonds, low fat cheese, yogurt, or veggies, he should not be given supplements unless prescribed by an avian vet. It is very important that a blood calcium test be performed at each annual exam, since calcium levels can change over time. Young birds will typically have a lower concentration than older companion birds.

A list of foods, showing the amount of calcium and phosphorus they contain, can be found in the article <u>Calcium, Phosphorus & Vitamin D3 in Your Bird's Diet</u>. The article also includes sources of Vitamin D3 and explains how calcium, phosphorus and Vitamin D3 must be balanced to ensure absorption and proper health.

A ratio of 2:1 calcium to available phosphorus in the diet, plus adequate Vitamin D, is recommended to ensure the proper amount of absorption of calcium by the body. If the bird is on a pelleted diet, a Vitamin D source is typically available. Vitamin D3 has the potential for toxicity and great caution is recommended when using a supplement that contains Vitamin D. Vitamin D3 is produced exclusively in the bird's body and is 30 to 40 times more potent than Vitamin D2 (a plant derivative) Ref. <u>Avian Medicine</u> page 83. Soft tissue mineralization, especially of the kidneys, is one of the toxic effects of excessive Vitamin D3. Ref. <u>Avian Medicine</u> pages 82, 84. Species susceptibility to toxic overdoses varies, as does susceptibility by sex.

Do not give your Grey pellets with added calcium or a calcium supplement unless it is medically necessary. Unnecessary and unneeded over-supplementation can lead to serious health complications, in companion Greys and in other birds.

Buying A Baby Grey: A Joint Responsibility

Nothing is more exciting than the impending purchase of a new baby Grey. However, excitement must be tempered with a commitment to purchase wisely. Below, several guidelines are discussed for the purchase of your new Grey. When prospective buyers adhere to these guidelines, two important goals are accomplished: They will choose healthy, well adjusted companions and they will set a humane standard for the conditions under which breeders raise and sell their babies.

The Breeding Environment

The breeder has an ethical responsibility to the breeding birds, the babies, and the buyer. Breeding birds deserve a clean pleasant aviary in which to reproduce including spacious cages and comfortable perches, clean water and nutritious food, and regular medical check-ups. Although breeders seldom permit visitors in the breeding facility (to avoid the disturbance a stranger can create), an unclean general environment probably means an unclean substandard aviary.

Since initially the well being of these creatures is totally dependent on the standard of care the breeder provides, the prospective buyer should carefully inspect the conditions under which the birds live before purchasing a baby Grey.

Babies deserve clean brooders and bedding, properly prepared food offered in abundance, suitable weaning cages, stimulating interactive toys, the companionship of siblings and humans, and a pleasant comfortable setting.

Babies have a right to the same meticulous and compassionate conditions described for breeding birds as well as regular feedings even when it is inconvenient to the handfeeder, regulated warmth and humidity, tender, considerate handling, ongoing socialization experiences, and a bountiful, individualized weaning program. In other words, quality breeders provide babies with a safe, healthy, simulating environment in which to grow and learn.

It is the responsibility of the breeder to maintain these standards of care resolutely, however, the buyer has a responsibility too: Don't buy your baby bird from those who don't maintain these standards. Before buying a baby, ask the breeder for references and talk to those whose opinion you respect regarding the aviary. Reputations are typically earned and should be scrutinized before choosing a breeder.

The Money Trap

Don't let price be your paramount consideration. With birds, as with other purchases, you mostly get what you pay for. It takes an enormous amount of time, effort, and money to maintain a quality aviary. If it is tempting to buy a baby whose "price is right", consider that no price is right enough if it costs the health of your existing collection or results in owning a baby that is sick or has poor pet potential. Breeders who invest their time and money assuring that the babies they sell are healthy, confident, loving birds are not able to offer a "great deal". Many breeders sell their baby birds just to support the rest of the flock. This allows them to continue an activity they deeply love and enjoy. Their biggest reward is the pleasure of turning over a healthy, happy baby to a caring, informed new owner.

The Unweaned Baby Trap

One common "great deal" to beware of is buying an unweaned baby. The fact of the matter is that sometimes it goes well and sometimes it doesn't. However, even when all goes well, getting a "great deal" on an unweaned Grey can end up being an expensive proposition. If the bird is young enough to require regulated warmth and humidity, you will have the additional expense of a brooder. Add to that the expense of handfeeding formula, syringes, disinfectant solutions, bedding, a thermometer, a gram scale, and a weaning cage.

In addition to the expense, one must account for the time and effort needed to properly raise an unweaned baby. Weeks or months of handfeeding will be required until the bird is weaned and there is no negotiating feeding schedules: Baby birds must be fed on a regular basis whether you have a dinner engagement or not. Time must be allocated each and every day to observe the baby, to maintain a clean environment, and to teach the baby how to be a bold and loving companion.

Money and time aside, the most compelling reason not to buy an unweaned baby is the staggering risks one assumes for the physical and emotional welfare of this precious creature. Those who sell unweaned babies are often neither willing nor able to offer support when you run into problems. There can be no guarantee on an unweaned baby. How can there be? There is no accounting for a buyer's level of knowledge or skill and thus no way to absolve him of the responsibility regarding a particular trauma. The mechanics of handfeeding may look simple enough but knowing (actually to sense even before the knowing) when a baby is in trouble and what action is required to swiftly resolve the danger is extremely difficult.

As a breeder I know what can happen to babies in inexperienced hands. I know of babies who were underfed and stunted. I know of babies who have suffered crop burn and life threatening bacterial and fungal infections. I know of babies who didn't wean until after they were are six months old or became chronic beggars or endure food trauma. The list goes on. Most importantly, I know what should be done to avoid these tragedies. Do you? Consider that even experienced handfeeders risk burning out a baby's crop or aspirating a baby. Obviously, the risk is that much greater with an inexperienced handfeeder.

We all have to decide what we are willing to allow in the quest for short-term monetary gain when we know, in the long run, doing so increases the chance of physical or emotional harm to our precious Grey babies.

Rationalizations and Myths

Too often people rationalize their desire to sell or buy unweaned babies with appealing but erroneous arguments such as, "Every handfeeder is a novice in the beginning." The important difference between novice handfeeders and breeder/handfeeders is one of ongoing experience: The novice handfeeder will always be a novice; the responsible breeder inevitably becomes an expert. We have no choice but to become expert at handfeeding. If we don't, our babies will be stunted, sick, or dead.

Burn every book that contains the statement: "Handfeeding your baby Grey is the only (or best) way for him to bond to you." This statement is not only totally false, it defies all logic as well. It is a myth to claim that a bird bonds only to (or even mostly to) those who feed him. What about the second and third and fourth and fifth and sixth hand birds out there? Who do they love? Do they only love the ones who handfed them when they were babies? There are an awful lot of "used" birds out there who love well and are well loved by

people who did not handfeed them. Perhaps the myth prevails, in part, because the owner feels a close bond to a creature that is totally dependent on him. This is a selfish motive and the change in handfeeders from the breeder to the buyer is a needlessly stressful, frightening event for the baby.

Another consideration is the way in which the ignorance or inexperience of the novice handfeeder can actually work against healthy bonding. Approaching the baby with anxiety and apprehension often results in anxious, apprehensive babies.

Reasons Not To Buy An Unweaned Baby

The following reasons not to buy an unweaned baby have been gathered over many years from the hard, painfully learned lessons of those who bought unweaned babies.

Most buyers don't know:

• Bacterial and fungal infections can result from poorly understood or applied principles of hygiene.

• Subtle or obvious signs or symptoms of illness or distress are not recognized or dealt with quickly enough.

• Weaning is a stressful time and the experiences during that time stay with a bird his whole life.

• A baby bird will eat scalding hot formula.

• A weaning baby can starve to death with food sitting in front of him.

• Water drinking is a learned behavior.

• The expiration date on each container of handrearing formula should be checked before purchase.

• Pressure on the beak of a handfeeding baby will deform the beak.

• Picking up a baby incorrectly can bruise the internal organs.

• Baby Greys are very particular about the temperature of the formula.

• The crop of a healthy baby bird should empty regularly, feeding after feeding, day after day, month after month.

• The weaning process begins weeks before a baby bird can sustain his weight without formula. Weaning is not an event. It is a very long process that begins at around six weeks of age with the initial offering of weaning foods.

Forced or Deprivation Weaning

Weaning is one of the most important periods in a bird's life and the effects of the methods employed are life long. A baby will suffer from improper weaning whether an ignorant, uncaring breeder or an ignorant, well-intentioned novice does it.

Babies can be gradually weaned according to their own timetable with bountiful, varied foods offered to full, contented tummies or they can be weaned by force or deprivation by abruptly withdrawing the handrearing formula according to some standard, fixed schedule. With force or deprivation weaning, babies are given no other alternative: They learn to eat on their own or they die.

A Grey who is weaned inappropriately or improperly will learn the wrong lessons regarding trust, love, security, and bonding when he is forced to eat independently, before he is ready, to save his own life. The baby learns that humans cannot be trusted to provide food. Such approaches to weaning teach baby Greys to be anxious about humans who they perceive as starving them. All of the developmental stages including opening of the eyes, feathering, perching, flying, food independence, and successful socialization are retarded by food deprivation. Too often force-weaned babies are headed for a long, sad journey from home to home and a dismal future.

Proponents of forced or deprivation weaning have no regard for the highly individual physical and psychological development of baby birds. Some will wean earlier than others; some will wean later than others. A hungry baby will not wean at all. A hungry baby will not give up waiting for formula. A hungry baby will refuse to waste waning energy exploring the weaning foods or attempting to discover which foods will satisfy his hunger. From the baby's perspective it is more efficient to wait and wait and wait for the handfeeder to relent.

In nature, parents will feed a juvenile as old as 6 months of age. With forced or deprivation weaning the goal is often for the baby to be "weaned" (that is, eating independently) by 10 or 11 weeks of age! How early must the deprivation begin to meet such a timeline? Baby birds who are "weaned" at 10 or 11 weeks are starved into eating what is provided to them instead of the high calorie formula they require at this age when they naturally begin to eat less. They will lose a massive amount of weight before they finally figure out that formula won't be forthcoming—that they better learn to eat what is provided or they will die.

The use of a forced or deprivation approach to food independence constitutes the harsh termination of handfeeding and is thus the antithesis of a weaning process. Weaning should be a gentle, loving, confidence building process. When a baby is forced or deprivation weaned, the cries, the digging, the restlessness, the anxious eyes will tell any compassionate person that the baby bird is hungry. The consequences of such an ignorant, cruel strategy are profound. The results are anxious, upset babies that grow into untrusting, unloving adults. Don't buy a baby that has been forced or deprivation weaned.

Bountiful Weaning

The weaning process is a stressful time for both the bird and the handfeeder. Like other animal babies, and like human babies, there are enormous individual differences among baby birds. Depending on such factors as general health, weight, and the age at which weaning foods are introduced, baby Greys wean comfortably and naturally when their internal clock tells them it is time to wean. For most, fledging and the true beginning of weaning usually occur at approximately the same time, around ten weeks. However, weaning will be delayed if a baby bird is starved in an effort to get him to eat independently. It is a dire misperception that a baby will eat when he is hungry enough.

The bountiful weaning method teaches baby birds to have three life long expectations:

• Trust in humans as the givers of nourishment and therefore life.

• Love for humans who provide warm comforting food on demand.

• Confidence that starvation and deprivation are not the norm associated with humans.

Trust, love, and confidence are much-desired traits in a companion bird which develop in the early weeks and months of life.

Bountiful weaning does not mean handfeeding a baby bird until he is 6 months old. It means providing weaning foods as early as 6 weeks of age. It means not starving a baby bird into food independence. It means understanding and accepting that a baby bird who is well fed will begin naturally refusing formula when the time is right for him and will wean easily without hunger, anxiety or trauma. Typically, this occurs anywhere from 12 to 16 weeks of age, but it takes an experienced breeder to recognize the window of developmental opportunity when food independence truly begins.

Question breeders about their weaning philosophy. Buy only from breeders who wean their babies bountifully to raise curious, confident, loving babies who can cope with life's inevitable demands and stresses. Avoid the "great deal" that invariably ends sadly. Take seriously your responsibility to shape the standards of care used by breeders of African Grey babies. Someone's bird is at stake.

Handfeeding, weaning, and socializing should be left to those who have the experience in these areas. If an experienced, knowing breeder does it, the baby bird will most likely stay in the home which has been carefully selected by the breeder. A well behaved, responsive, trusting, tame bird will love well and be a well loved, intimate, permanent member of the family. That is what I want for you and your baby and for all the babies.

Your Baby Grey Is Coming Home
A Letter to My Babies' New *Parronts*

It is vitally important to be patient, gentle, and considerate of your new Grey. He doesn't know you. He is in a strange place with strangers. He will undergo a brief grieving period. He has lost all that was familiar and loved - the other babies he played with and his beloved and trusted caregiver.

The adjustment, as far as food, cage, and toys are concerned, should be a brief one. It will take a little longer for him to know and trust you. The bird-human relationship is based on love and trust and this takes time to develop. Without love and trust, there can be no relationship.

Early Environmental Management

Your new Grey bird may be cautious and watchful during the early days and weeks. He will want to learn the lay of the land and adjust to the new sights and sounds of your home. He will need to adjust to your other birds (if any) and other companion animals you may have. Because of careful early management, he will be inclined toward acceptance, but don't assume it. A bird is not a domesticated companion animal and all who wish to have a satisfactory relationship with him must earn his trust and love.

If you have other companion animals, keep them quiet or away from him for the first few weeks - because of safety considerations and because the bird needs time and space to adjust to the presence of predator animals. Don't overload him with too much confusion or noise. If you have children or grandchildren, caution them about running up to the cage, gesturing wildly, speaking loudly, or screaming. Birds often are frightened of children because of their abrupt activity, sudden noise, and impulsiveness. Adult family members should be cautioned to avoid sudden movements or speaking in a loud voice.

The adjustment period should last about three weeks. Be patient. Don't rush him. He doesn't know how loved he is and how anxiously awaited he was. Hold down the excitement. Be calm. Allow him time. Let him explore the cage and become familiar with it. The toys will be new and exciting and he will want to check them out. He will accept you but he must be given time to do so. He needs to become comfortable - with you and his new environment. The care you take in the early weeks and months will pay a rich dividend.

Prior to using a noisy appliance like a nut chopper, a blender, an ice crusher, a vacuum or steam cleaner, call out "BIG noise."

"Biiiiig noise". I warn my babies before using any of these noisy appliances and they are accustomed to hearing a potentially scary noise just after the warning. I call out the warning, turn the appliance on and then off immediately, and then warn them again so they know which loud or scary noise will be heard after the final warning.

Don't invite the family or neighbors over to see him just yet. Let him come to know you. Be careful to avoid accidents - take your time. Try not to let any "bad" things happen. Once he knows and trusts you, he will be able to accept an accident as just that. Hold him securely. Don't let him fall or be off balance when on your hand or knee. Don't push him into accepting intimate petting until he is ready.

Arrange for your baby Grey to come home at a time when you will have a weekend or several days with him. Get your annual vacation out of the way before you bring him home. If you must go away for a weekend trip, take him with you. Don't leave him home alone or board him for at least the first year.

Remember he is just a baby and will need more sleep and more food than an adult bird. If you have a sleep cage, use it so he will have undisturbed sleep. Give him all the food he will eat. He will not get fat. He has weight to put back on after weaning. He should have food available at all times. Weigh him daily for at least the first 6 months. Record the weight. Learn what is normal for your Grey - there will be small weight changes over time. Small losses – a downward trend for several days will call for a trip to the avian vet. He should be seen by the vet immediately if there is a large loss on any one day.

To accustom your Grey to variety in shapes, colors, sizes, and textures, it is important that he be exposed to small quantities of pellets other than the base pellet you have chosen. Samples are readily available from most of the bird food companies. Put a teaspoon or so of one of the sample pellets in with the base pellet. He may like one sample pellet better than another. Experiment to see which of the sample pellets he likes. There is no need to buy a large quantity; you may find he hates the sample. The pellets I recommend as a base pellet are Harrison's, Hagen's and Ziegler's.

If your new cage has an adjustable grate on the bottom of the cage, position the grate at the higher position in the beginning. If he takes a tumble, he won't have so far to fall. Some birds are paper chewers. If your bird is a paper chewer, leave the grate at the higher position permanently so that he doesn't have access to the waste tray. If the cage doesn't have an adjustable grate, pad the grate with a towel or old blanket. Put a piece of newspaper over the padding. He should be familiar enough with the cage not to fall after a few days. Babies who are allowed to learn to fly are sure-footed, agile, and confident. It will be unusual for them to fall.

Bathe your Grey daily. He should become

accustomed to being bathed each morning but as long as he has time to dry before bedtime, he can be bathed at other times. An early introduction to bathing is very important. I begin spray bathing the babies when they are partially feathered – around six weeks of age.

Never leave your bird alone with other companion animals. Never allow the slightest physical contact with another companion animal. In any confrontation, the bird always loses....eventually. The bird is fearless, he doesn't know his life may be in grave danger. Cage or crate other companion animals when you are away if these animals have the free rein of the house. They should never have access to the room where the bird is caged - whether you are home or away.

The Importance of Trustbuilding

Greys are, I believe, motivated by fear and escape. The companion animals to which you are accustomed are not so motivated. Therefore, the most important order of business is the building of trust. Trust is fragile. However, the longer the trust "agreement" between you and your Grey is unbroken, the sturdier it is.

Our birds are clipped for their safety and are unable to escape when their natural fear overcomes their trust in us and in the safety of their environment. The bird's association with humans must be exclusively gentle, loving, kind, and positive. Each positive interaction proves to the bird that humans are understanding and trustworthy caretakers. My baby birds have the history with me that all outcomes are positive and praiseworthy but this history must be developed individually with each new human they encounter. Trust building human behavior and a history of positive outcomes with humans adds to the bird's database of trust and enhances

the companionship potential that exists in these intelligent and sensitive birds. In this way, fear can be dropped to a lower order of importance and your bird's personality can blossom in a trusting and secure human environment.

The Consequences of Punishing Management

What are some of the human behaviors that should be avoided if we are to neutralize fear and establish a critically important atmosphere of security and trust?

• Isolation as a tool for behavior modification.

• Laddering as an exercise in dominance or as punishment.

• Jerky or unpredictable movements.

• Unsteady, too large, or too slippery perches.

• Dropping the bird to the floor.

• "Earthquaking" or shaking the bird.

Trust building human behavior and a history of positive outcomes will result in a calmer and less fearful personality.

- Slapping the cage.

- Glaring.

- Hitting the beak.

- Covering the cage during non-sleep time.

- Shouting.

- Forcing the bird to do something he does not want to do.

Do any of these things and I will guarantee that your sweet bird will no longer be sweet. Most of these punitive techniques are designed to deal with biting. Biting is not a natural behavior. Grey birds swiftly learn that biting is one of the quickest ways to get through to humans who ignore or fail to understand what is to the bird a reasonable or normal preference. Learned biting can be difficult to overcome because it has become a first reaction rather than a last resort. Therefore, all reasonable measures must be taken to avoid teaching a bird to bite. Biting is and should be a last ditch option and employed only when a bird has no other way to "tell" us he doesn't like something that is happening. A gradually accumulated history of positive interactions is the way to avoid a biting Grey.

The well researched side effects of aversive or painful or punitive punishment across species are:

- Withdrawal from all interactions with the punisher.

- Reduction in overall responding.

- Escalation or an increase in aggressive behavior.

- Becoming fearful of anything that is related to or similar to the punishing situation or person

- Increasing another negative behavior or displaying unwanted behavior at a high rate

in another place or circumstance.

Sound familiar? These are commonly seen behavioral responses when dominance-based management is used to affect the conduct of a Grey.

Only benign punishment may be used. An example of benign punishment is to calmly and persistently remove the bird from your shoulder when he "misbehaves"; i.e., making holes in your clothes, chewing on jewelry or ears, pulling your hair, etc. He can be removed for a period of ten seconds with the "Up" request, placed on a nearby t-stand, and then returned to your shoulder with "OK". Greys are a safe bird for shoulder sitting and many enjoy it immensely. They like the closeness to the beloved one. Teach him that "OK" means he is allowed to sit on or return to your shoulder. Constantly praise him when he is demonstrating the behaviors that you would like repeated in the future. This is how to train a bird.

The One Person Grey

To permit the narrowing of the life experience to one person goes counter to the Grey family or flock ethic. While there is a favored person in the life of most companion animals, it is reasonable to expect that our companion birds will be at least civil to other kind, gentle, and understanding adult family members. The relationship that a bird will permit has to be accepted without hurt feelings on the part of the less favored family members

Games people play:

- Passing the bird from one family member's hand to another family member's hand with lots of praise for courage and civility.

- The favored person can facilitate civil relationships with others by praising the bird lavishly for being accepting of the attentions of others.

• The less favored family members can offer the bird treats. It is important for the less favored to be calm and gentle, as the bird will have less tolerance for a "bad" experience.

• The less favored family members should approach the bird with the hands held behind the back and speak softly and reassuringly.

Gateway Management

Allow your Grey to come out of the cage on his own if he is reluctant to step up for you in the early days. Learning to trust a different hand than the one he was accustomed to may take several days.

It is of no consequence if your Grey bird is "higher" than you. Greys like to be up high. They should be allowed to perch on the top of their cage playpens since there are no height dominance issues. The motivation for perching in a high spot is safety, not dominance with your Grey. They feel safer when they have a 360 degree view of their world. The need for safety is biologically hard wired. I have to stand on tiptoe to retrieve my nine year old male Grey from atop his cage toy holder and he has never failed to step up for me.

My babies are praised each and every time, without fail, they step up or down for me. Stepping up or down is such an easy form of communication to establish and the result of stepping up and down is always positive for my babies. Your Grey will expect to hear praise and expect that nothing "bad" will happen when he steps up or down. Often my babies' first words are "good bird" because they have heard it so often.

Watch his body language carefully. He may

Some babies may allow you to hold their toes using light pressure with your thumb.

be unwilling for you to pin his toes. Some are more accepting than others. Some babies will accept pinning from me but not from the new owner. If the bird nips at your fingers during transport when you pin his toes or indicates he is unwilling for you to pin his toes, don't do it during the early days and weeks. He may be more accepting later. Make sure he is balanced and steady on your hand. Take a few seconds to have him come out of the cage on the "up" request. If he doesn't step up promptly, pick up the two long front toes on one of his feet, brace his weight under his foot on your forefinger, and lift him straight up slowly. The other foot will come up. Some youngsters will step up more willingly if both hands are held palm up prior to him stepping up. I do this as a signal to a baby that I want him to step onto my hand. When you are returning him to a perch, before saying "down", place his tail behind the perch. He will step backward onto the perch. Never let go of one foot until the other foot is securely on the perch.

My babies have never experienced human aggression of any kind. Everything that they have learned has been taught with kindness and love. The worst thing you can do would be to take one of these Greys, or any bird for that matter, and begin to employ a dominance-based form of management. This will significantly impact your bird's behavior, make his life miserable, and seriously reduce his suitability as a companion bird.

Grey parrots aren't devious, manipulative, arrogant, or any of the characteristics that are sometimes used to describe bird behavior. These are wild animals one generation out of Africa who will do what pleases them, and one thing that pleases every wild animal is to feel safe and protected.

So, if they are to also do what pleases you, you must make it worth their while. Praise, approval, acceptance, love, gentleness, and understanding are the key to a "good" companion bird and it is these things that will make a bird want to please you. Aggression, however natural it may be to the human

animal, will never work. Birds will not and cannot adjust to this type of interaction. YOU are the one who must adjust to living with a bird.

We can't influence everything when it comes to behavior. Some behaviors are hardwired. And that which cannot be influenced must be worked around. The range of behaviors that can be influenced is vast and supported by a well-documented body of science. Most importantly, that body of science has shown that behavior can be influenced with gentle, kind, loving methods. Positive, caring, and supportive understanding works as well with birds as it does with friends, kids, and husbands.

Your Grey will guide you in what he is willing to accept. The care you take early on will pay handsome dividends later. Be aware. Watch carefully. Follow his lead. And you will be the parront this sweet baby bird deserves.

Socializing The African Grey

The Early Days

A happy, well-adjusted, and trusting Grey is the product of a breeder or handfeeder who understands Greys; who provides a calm and reassuring environment; who is willing to take the time to guide this young life along the path to acceptance and understanding of the idea that humans are kind, gentle, and loving. Socialization starts long before a bird is weaned and takes considerable time and effort by the breeder or handfeeder. Breeders who don't have the time or the knowledge to socialize a baby Grey often produce birds that make "poor" companions. They are also the ones who will sell unweaned baby Greys to retail clients or other inexperienced handfeeders.

This winning lineup shows well-adjusted, socialized babies from different clutches.

Socializing is such an indescribable art. The techniques that work for me come from years of experience. Breeders or others who sell unweaned Greys often don't have the time or the knowledge to assist the pet owner in socializing or weaning the new bird. If a breeder or pet store only sells unweaned birds, how can they know what needs to be done to ensure the baby becomes a well behaved, gentle, and loving companion? I wish it was as easy as do "x" and then do "y" and then "z". But it's not. Successful socializing of a Grey is an art. It is more an attitude, a frame of mind, an internal temperament.

An inexperienced owner may not understand the systematic methods one needs to employ to ensure that baby Greys are properly fed, socialized, and weaned. The problems associated with any temporary "acting out" or early rebellion can be understood and avoided with the assistance of an experienced and knowledgeable breeder who sells weaned babies. If the baby is properly managed from the earliest weeks of life by an experienced breeder or handfeeder, problems with unwanted behavior will be temporary and associated with coming of age. The first two years of a Grey's life are crucial for the evolution of the adult bird that is comfortable living with humans. It is important that unwanted behavior in young birds be dealt with promptly and properly without aggression or attempts to dominate the bird. Aggressive human behavior is frightening to Greys and human attempts to dominate can create very serious behavior problems in them.

These are of some of the techniques I have discovered which work for me and for my Grey babies. Is all of it necessary? I don't know. I only know they work for me.

I love and respect my babies very much and I think they know that. I am never rushed or impatient with them. I am always very gentle and reassuring. As an example: the youngest baby in a recent clutch was easily startled when I reached for him to handfeed him. Over several days, I talked to him softly without touching him, put my face close to him, kissed his beak, and asked him if he was ready to eat. It only took a few days for him to stop being startled or pulling away when I reached for him.

My babies are never handled roughly. They are always supported so that they are never in fear of falling. I pick them up for feeding from the rear, cupping their feet and rear on the palms of my open hands. If you pick them up from the front, they will scoot their rear over the tips of your fingers. They feel much more secure when they are picked up from the rear. After a few weeks, the babies will actually turn their backs and shuffle their clumsy feet sideways into the palms of my hands. I approach their feet from the side and they shuffle into the slightly cupped palms of my hands.

Before I remove the babies from the brooder, I softly cluck to them and tell them what is going to happen. They don't like the opening of the brooder door at first, but soon start heading toward me when I come to feed them. I place my hands under the wings on the babies' sides. Soon they are lifting their wings when I reach for them. My Grey babies don't clutch tightly with their feet and

talons when they are being transported or when they are perching on my hand. They quickly learn they won't be allowed to fall. As I spoonfeed, I take advantage of that opportunity to put my hand on the back of the head, on top of the head, on their backs. Sometimes I cover their eyes and their heads (except for the beak) completely with my hand. I always clasp them softly and gently. I want to accustom them to being touched.

As they become older, I use a hot damp paper towel on their backs, wings and tails after I wipe their beaks. I spread the wings, wipe off the wings, the top and the underside of the tail. This is a way to accustom them to touch and the handling of the wings and the tail.

The babies in the weaning cage all come tumbling to the door when I open it. When I sit beside the cage, they come to the sides so I can tickle under the jaw and pet their beaks. What I see in my babies are outgoing assertive birds, interested in exploring, curious, attracted to the new food in the dish and the new toys.

I begin misting my baby Greys when the

flight and tail feathers start emerging. There should be no reason for a Grey to hate and fear being misted, provided they are exposed to baths from a very young age. An older bird may not like his bath, but this fear can be avoided by very early bathing or misting. This early misting, especially of the flight and tail feathers, at a very early age will avoid marks on the feathers. Most often these "stress" marks are caused by the ends of the keratin sheath rubbing against the feather as they grow farther and farther out of the sheath. That likely accounts for the regularity of the marks since the feathers grow at a pre-determined rate. This is not to say that "stress" marks aren't present on the feathers during illness or from a lack of food (crop down-time or a skipped feeding). It's just more likely the marks are from the sheath rubbing against the feather. The initial feathers seem to be more fragile and more easily damaged than adult plumage.

The socialization techniques change slightly when they are older since reassurance has made their natural fear of humans a non-issue, but handling and talking to them very frequently during the day doesn't change. I catch the babies' eyes and talk to them each time I pass the cage. I kiss and pet them during feeding and when they are playing or taking naps on the tops of their cages. It takes a lot of time. Retail buyers of unweaned Greys don't realize just how time consuming it is to prepare a Grey for a permanent home with a satisfied client. A well socialized Grey baby is gentle, endearing, and trusting.

The temperament, behavior, and attitude of baby Greys are, in significant ways, determined by the handfeeder. However, each Grey is an individual and there can be dramatic differences even in siblings. There is a wide range of personalities in Greys, just as in humans. By and large, except perhaps for their intelligence and sensitivity, Grey babies are like other birds and require a calm, secure, and comfortable environment.

Greys are one of the quietest birds—well suited for the home. Some do learn obnoxious sounds. Microwave beeps, run-down smoke alarm battery beeps, truck backup beeps, telephone rings, answering machine beeps, pager beeps, piercing wolf whistles, unpleasant vocalizations from other birds, etc. The key is to avoid exposing them to these undesirable sounds. And that's not always easy.

When baby birds are exposed to change, variety, color, movement, and toys from the early weeks of life, they come to view these things as normal and nothing to be afraid of or concerned about. The de-sensitization of Grey babies, as well as babies of other species, begins at the beginning.

These vitally important issues make a compelling case for the pet owner to buy his well-fed, properly socialized, bountifully weaned Grey from a quality breeder or pet store who sells only weaned babies. Carefully interview the seller. Understand the early crucial events that affect the bird's life. A decision of this importance requires careful research. Together we can close the revolving door that so many birds experience—from home to home to home.

Early Socialization: A Biological Need and the Key to Companionability

By Bobbi Brinker and S. G. Friedman, PhD.

Since the dawn of psychology, no subject has stirred more continuous and widespread interest than the relative influence of heredity versus environment on human behavior. From philosophers to parents, most of us have speculated about which force is stronger when "Nature" and "Nurture" are thrown into the ring. This subject is equally relevant to the behavior of parrots, in that it impacts our choice of best practices with which to facilitate their full potential as companions.

Related Research

Speculation not withstanding, research in the fields of psychology and education strongly suggests that environment plays a highly significant role in the development of all three behavior domains: mental, social, and emotional. Experiments in the 1950s showed that baby monkeys who were raised without their parents or other nurturing caregivers stared blankly for abnormally long periods of time and rocked back and forth hugging themselves unnaturally when confronted with stressful events. Sadly, the very same pattern of behavior is reported by psychologists working with children who spent the first year of their lives without nurturing care in Romanian orphanages in the late 1980s. However, no research has been more startling or conclusive than recent finds from the field of neuroscience.

With recent technological advances, in particular brain imaging, scientists have discovered that the electrical (neural) activity of brain cells actually changes the physical

Tactile and visual stimulation is important in the proper development of baby greys.

structure of the brain. And, what produces such neural activity? Experience. Furthermore, although a human baby is born with all the nerve cells (neurons) it will ever have, the brain produces trillions more connections (synapses) in the first year of life than it will ever use. Remarkably, those synapses that are not stimulated by early sensory experiences are "pruned" by the brain and eliminated. Therefore, the more environmental stimulation a baby experience, the more synapses are maintained. Ultimately, the remaining synapses provide the connections between neurons that result in the unique pattern with which each individual brain is "wired".

This research demonstrates that it is not only the outward behavior of children that is affected by environments deprived of stimulation and nurturing care but the physical structure of their brains as well. These findings have been widely replicated with many different species of animals, including cats and rats and even fruit flies. Still, it is likely that there will always be more questions than answers when entering this "hall of mirrors" where nature and nurture interact. Conclusions from these studies should be drawn carefully, as the exact nature of the relationship between the number of brain synapses and specific behaviors remains largely unknown. However, even with this caveat in mind, current science from varied fields does converge to suggest the following: 1) learning is a biological need, and 2) the quantity and quality of early experiences affect future learning potential and social/emotional behavior.

Relevance to Companion Parrots

Although we are not aware of research specifically imagining the neonatal brains of parrots, generalization of the above findings is clearly justified. We can think of no characteristics specific to companion parrots that would make these two conclusions invalid. Based on the scientific data and the experiences of many people who raise successful companion birds, it is reasonable to expect that baby parrots have a similar biological need to learn and that they too are negatively affected by a lack of environmental stimulation and nurturing care during their early development.

These conclusions make a compelling case for the early socialization of pet parrots. Socialization is the process by which baby birds are taught to successfully live in the human environment with humans as their primary companions. Early socialization begins at the moment the baby is removed from the nest box and continues in various forms for the rest of the bird's life. The objective of early socialization is to teach two categories of behavior: 1) behaviors required for companionability, and 2) behaviors that ensure the bird's comfort, health and hap-

piness. The art of early socialization is in the ability to arrange as much overlap between the two categories as possible so that what is required is also what makes birds happy.

From the earliest weeks babies should be offered brightly colored hanging toys to joust with and floor toys to beak. They should be moved to various locations to get different perspectives of the world. They should be given the opportunity to interact with other birds; play with water; step up and down; explore foods that vary in color, shape and texture; listen to music; glide to the floor; walk on flat surfaces; meet strangers; hear vacuums; beat their wings; peek out of boxes; hang upside-down from ropes; ride in baskets; somersault; feel human breath and warm hands; and see children giggling - just to name a few socialization activities.

Early socialization is a purposeful, labor-intensive process in which the babies are saturated with rich experiences and delivered at the appropriate time and optimal pace for each individual bird. It requires facilitators – mentors who maximize each bird's companionability by fulfilling their natural need to learn. The result is birds that are more trusting, confident, independent, curious, and flexible in all aspects of their lives.

The Bird Mill Crisis

These recent breakthroughs in the scientific community regarding the relationship between experience and behavior offer an oasis of validation to those who suspected as much all along. Now we wonder: How much more research is needed to persuade those involved in bird mill breeding and raising of parrots that their practices are inadequate if not inhumane?

People who "mill" birds typically have a particular belief system. Bird millers believe that baby birds are merchandise, goods, or wares, to be bought and sold like any other product or commodity. Consequently, they believe that their baby bird business is subject to the very same laws and practices as the business of garden hoses or toothpaste. They resent the notion that their profit motive necessarily conflicts with the humane and enriched raising of companion parrots. Bird millers provide unstimulating, unnurturing environments to the baby birds they produce. They do so because it is cost efficient, and that is, simply, their bottom line. It does not pay to do otherwise. In fact, it is so patently true that since the raising of properly weaned, well-socialized babies does not yield a significant profit, it seems prudent to be wary of buying birds from people who think that it should.

Another characteristic of bird mill breeders is their interest in selectively breeding the "Perfect Pet Parrot." Certainly the practice of responsible animal husbandry is relevant to the successful breeding of companion

Baby greys need space, stimulation, and individual attention. Bird mills cannot provide this.

birds. However, the "traits" often targeted for elimination by bird millers are not necessarily the result of errant genes. We believe them to be learned behaviors that are exhibited due to a lack of environmental stimulation, socialization, and nurturing care. Unfortunately, it is within the realm of possibility to selectively breed the silent cockatoo, the insensitive grey, and the still macaw, but what will be lost in the process of "de-parroting" these birds is unimaginable. The essential message is that selective breeding is not an acceptable solution for the very problem behaviors that bird mill practices create.

Here is our list of "Top 10" bird mill practices to avoid when selecting the person from whom to buy your baby bird. Only one of them needs to be true for you to turn away and look elsewhere.

• Breeding pairs are treated as egg factories for artificial incubation.
• Babies are confined to small stacking brooders or cages at all times except for feeding.
• Babies are kept in empty cages devoid of interesting toys or other stimulation.
• Babies are kept in nursery rooms isolated from essential human contact and contact with each other.
• Babies are fed as quickly and as infrequently as possible with timesaving but unnurturing techniques such as gavage or power feeding.
• Babies have little or no instruction or exploration time with humans or each other.
• Babies are sold very young or unweaned to inexperienced pet owners with no inquiry regarding the suitability of a particular

home, a particular species, or a particular baby.

• Little or no instruction or educational information is provided to the buyer.
• No after-sale care is offered or provided.
• The breeder talks a lot about genetically arranging the perfect pet bird.

Improving the Odds

In light of our unequivocal criticism of bird mill practices, we must take care not to condemn the birds that were so raised. We must also support the people who bought their parrots during the time when there was a dearth of good, detailed information about raising, selecting, and living with companion parrots. Perhaps even more detrimental than the lack of information was the preponderance of misinformation that is now, thankfully, being corrected. Given the complexity and intelligence of parrots, it is likely that to some degree we will always be "wishing we knew then what we know now." Surely we can improve the future of companion birds and their owners without giving up on the birds raised in the past.

It is also true that some birds have beaten the bird mill odds to become fabulous companions. Their resilience may be partially due to interspecies differences, as well as individual differences within a species. Either way, it is a testimony to the parrot spirit, their nurturing families and an undeniable measure of good luck.

Unfortunately, many more birds suffer the lack of early socialization by exhibiting predictable behavior deficits, such as poor physical coordination; an inability to entertain themselves with toys; narrow, unhealthy food preferences; excessive fear; unpredictable aggression; chronic biting; and incessant screaming. These can be difficult behaviors to eliminate, but even the

most challenging problems may be reduced. There are now many excellent behavior consultants, Internet sites and mail lists, innovative strategies such as clicker training, and written materials to help you improve the bird mill odds.

Although it is never too late for your bird to benefit from the process of socialization, the best approach is problem prevention through early socialization delivered by knowledgeable, experienced breeders. It is not the buyer's responsibility to do the work that prepares a bird for a lifetime of companionability with humans.

The Solution

The real decision-makers about the way baby birds will be raised are neither the bird millers nor the responsible, knowledgeable breeders. As is typical with commerce, it is the consumer who holds the power to ultimately decide. With increased awareness, we can choose to buy baby birds that are raised in ways that are consonant with the current knowledge about brain and behavior development to maximize their companionability.

We are on the brink of a new dawn in psychology as neuroscience and related disciplines reveal groundbreaking information about the interaction among environment, brain structure, and behavior. Still, enough is known right now about the interaction between nature and nurture to give us confidence in our choice of best practices with which to raise successful companion parrots. Scientific evidence combined With years of experience from competent breeders validates the assertion that early socialization is the key to happy, companionable birds. This is, of course, in the best interest of the pet owners but more importantly, it is in the best interest of the birds.

Life After Weaning - I
Your Companion Bird and You

Owning a bird is one of the most rewarding experiences a person can have. But like all things that are worth doing, it is worth doing well. Birds are very special beings. They are blessed with a high level of intelligence and capable of enriching their owner's lives in hundreds of ways. The owner who takes the time to understand this specialness and treats his bird with gentleness, compassion, and love will be rewarded with joy, love, trust, and an unforgettable relationship in return.

I've worked with birds for many years and have tried to see the world from the bird's view. A loving parental relationship, based upon gentle interaction, perceptiveness and consideration of a bird's reality are the key. If you want a gentle bird, he must be treated gently and with consideration. Not only is a bird a lifetime companion but he can and will learn his whole life. Cast yourself as the parental figure and deal with your bird consistently, fairly, and gently.

Birds, like other prey animals, can be suspicious and cautious in a new situation. They are not domesticated animals. They are, in most instances, one generation removed from the wild. Inborn and inbred instincts are fully intact. Birds, unlike some other animals, don't live only in the moment. Their curiosity, intelligence, memory, and emotions are shaped by the past. They think differently, but that difference is not inferior.

Birds are amoral—they feel no regret after eating your computer keyboard or dismantling your mouse. They cannot be shamed into "good" behavior. They are what they are, albeit tame, loving, and trusting with those they respect and love. This love and

respect must be earned—it won't come in a day, a week, or perhaps even a month, but it will come.

Beginning Your Relationship

Initially move slowly and perform needed tasks around him deliberately. If an item must be carried past him, hold the item below waist level. Talk softly and reassuringly, make frequent eye contact. Every time you pass the cage, speak to him; it can be nonsense, the tone is all important.

Socialization, in many ways, comes from the emotions and the mind of the handfeeder or owner. When dealing with birds, the harmony of your interior emotions and external actions will be reflected in the behavior of your bird. Never approach a bird quickly or with excitement. If you are anxious, in a hurry, impatient—stop, breathe deeply and allow your emotions to subside. Birds are empathic and very sensitive creatures who pick up on your emotions.

After a settling-in period, begin more extensive and intensive touching. The head, nape, under the wings, and toes are the areas they are accustomed to have petted. Some birds like to have their toes gently squeezed and massaged. Another benefit is the added sense of security they feel when perched on the hand. You will be better able to control the bird if you "pin" the toes. Some birds do not accept pinning from the new owner and careful attention should be paid to the bird's reaction to pinning the toes.

It is important for the owner to initiate frequent interaction. This avoids the sight of a bird clinging to the bars of the cage calling for attention. If the bird is spoken to and acknowledged dozens of times a day, he won't feel it necessary to resort to what may become unpleasant efforts to gain your attention.

Many short periods of attention are more desirable than one or two long sessions. The short interactions are, by nature, on an irregular schedule. Irregularity is part of the necessary conditioning so that the bird doesn't come to expect a certain amount of attention at any one particular time. If you will take the time to do these things in a conscious manner, the payoff will be a bird that knows he is loved and cherished because he has seen so many examples of your love.

Be considerate. If the bird is eating, grooming, napping, playing or otherwise safely occupied, wait until you catch his eye and say in a coaxing manner: "Would you like to come with me?" or "Would you like your head scratched?" If you interrupt in a questioning manner, he likely will want a ride or a tickle. Don't feel rejected if he prefers to continue his present activity. Don't expect him to give up an enjoyable activity unless he wants to do so.

Defining The Roles

A bird needs to understand what is expected from him as well as what he can expect. All companion animals are comfortable with reasonable limits and reasonable predictable behavior from their human companions. "Y" action from the bird produces "C" behavior from the human.

Once the bird accepts the owner as the guide, the teacher, the parental figure, the mentor, both of you can be comfortable in your home and the space you share. The relationship is not master/slave. A bird will never be able to accept that because it presupposes the bird will behave perfectly within the "master's" limits. Unlike any other companion animal, birds can be themselves (parrots), be true to their identity as individuals, and still have a warm, deep, satisfying, parental relationship with those they love and trust.

Speaking softly to a bird and slowly putting your head around the corner and saying, "I seeeeee you..." reassures him that the flock is nearby and he's not alone. Birds understand the concept that a thing or person still exists even though it is not in view. Calling softly to the bird in reply to a contact call reassures the bird he's still in touch with the flock. At first the bird will need a little more reassurance since he is in a strange place with strangers.

The Three Major Roles

There are three things the bird should learn: he should not bite without a reason, he should step "Up" and "Down" when requested, and he will not be permitted to roam the house.

Biting and Other Behaviors

You can encourage certain behaviors with treats but, as with other animals, praise and love will set a better tone for your future relationship.

Never strike your bird's beak with anything. Don't grab the bird's beak, some species recognize this as aggression on your part. Learning a bird's body language and avoiding situations when he will bite is far preferable to constant correction.

Some advocate potentially dangerous and psychologically damaging techniques for dealing with objectionable behavior in birds. Never drop your bird to the floor when he bites. Birds have hollow bones which makes this physically dangerous and sends a devastating psychological message. How can your bird trust you if you drop him to the floor?

Do not use the cage as a punishment area. Do not put your bird in a carrier or small cage in a remote location as punishment. Do not put your bird in a bathtub or shower stall as punishment. Do not cover the cage as punishment.

Another bad technique is the "earthquake" in which you drop the hand/arm the bird is sitting on several inches and wobble him when he is doing a forbidden thing. Once again, the bird will not feel safe or secure if you "earthquake" him. We have overcome the inborn reluctance to feeling safe on the floor with our domestic babies. Using a technique that leads your bird to think he is falling does nothing to build trust. Your clipped bird can't fly away to avoid injury.

A good technique for controlling birds that go after buttons, zippers, rings, etc. is to place your bird on your knee. Be persistent in discouraging this behavior. Rather than a bird hearing a steady stream of "No" "No" "No", it's better to ignore what he's doing. Move the forbidden item from his reach and instead, offer him a hand toy. The connection between the hand toy and the forbidden activity should not be obvious or the bird will perceive the hand toy as a reward for the forbidden activity.

Fingers are always forbidden. Even when the babies are just exploring, I seem not to notice but gently remove my finger from their beaks and offer a bit of food, a toy, a kiss, or a rub on the outside of the beak. Beaks are very sensitive and birds often enjoy this type of touching.

NEVER strike a bird no matter the provocation. They will neither forgive nor forget. Birds' bodies, with their hollow bones throughout, are equipped for flight, not fight. A domestic baby who has known only love and gentleness may never recover from physical punishment or punitive aloneness. It may break the spirit of the more fragile; in most it will produce an aggressive biting bird that fears that he will die with each confrontation.

Never tease your bird. No roughness, no rowdy behavior, no tug-of-war or ruffling the feathers the wrong way except on the head, nape, under the jaw.

Stepping Up and Down

Most domestic baby birds have a rudimentary awareness of concept of "Up" and "Down" learned from the breeder. Teach your bird to step up by saying "Up" and gently pushing your hand into his lower belly. If he doesn't step onto your hand, you can pick up the two front toes on either foot, support his weight with your hand, and lift the bird slowly and gently straight up. Repeat "Up" and praise him when he raises his other foot onto your hand. Say "Up" cheerfully, not loudly or sternly.

Bring your bird out of the cage on "Up". The cage is his home but you as the parental figure have a right to enter his "home" without objection from him.

When he is returned to his cage or placed on a play area or a stand, say "Down". Place the bird's tail behind the perch and never let go of the second foot until the first foot is securely on the perch. He will step off in a backward fashion and he depends on you to see that he is safely on the perch before you relinquish your hold.

Territory

The bird needs to learn that his territory is defined to be: on you, on his cage, in his cage, or on the play area. The young ones will have to be returned to these areas 10,000 times the first year. It may be inconvenient at times to enforce this rule, but it must be done for safety's sake. A bird only needs to be electrocuted once. Be matter-of-fact but replace the bird unless he comes directly to you—no side trips to chew on the baseboards. The bird is coming to you because he loves you and this should not be discouraged. The young one explores because his instincts tell him that his survival depends on knowing his environment.

A bird perceives all he can see as his territory. A bird that is exposed to all areas of the house is intelligent enough to realize that he cannot "defend" the whole house. Using this strategy can significantly reduce the territorial imperative. A bird exposed to many new safe experiences, locations, and people will be a self-confident, unafraid bird.

Touching

When you begin touching, do so very softly and gently. A bird fears and is intimidated by a heavy touch. Birds must be gently led to accept touching on the back and the long feathers on the wings because they are helpless to escape (fly away) from a predator while being so constrained.

I begin touching the babies from the first feeding using a very gentle touch, barely touching the body. In the beginning, I gently cup the bird's body while holding the sides of his jaws when he is being handfed. When they are a little older, I stroke them from above the nares in a soft gently cupping motion over the back of the body down to the tail. Even then they squirm and wiggle and it takes many weeks for them to accept this touching. When the birds are a little older, I begin placing both palms on the sides of the body under the wings, raise the wings and kiss the back between the wings. I also raise the wings and kiss the side of the body.

Don't attempt these intimacies at first but begin to let the bird know through soft words and a reassuring attitude that he can come to expect pleasure from you. Go a little past his comfort zone. Then stop, still talking and reassuring him. Return to the touches he accepts readily. Don't touch the areas he's uncomfortable with for several hours. Go slow, as you won't regret the time taken later. Pay very close attention when you go beyond his comfort level and stop before he reacts. Done correctly with attention to his body language and comfort level, you will have a loving, confiding, responsive companion.

When the bird bows his head and ruffles his head and nape, he can be petted from nape to forehead (against the way the feathers grow). The head, nape, and jaw area are the only areas the feathers should be petted against the grain.

"Peek-a-boo" games with a towel on a bed can be beneficial. The towel should cover the owner's face rather than the bird's head in the first phase of the game. This game should initially be from the front and can progress to the bird standing on the towel and the towel being brought up over the bird's head, first from the front and then from the back. The towel should be opened slowly so the bird can see the owner's face and hear the cue "peek-a-boo".

Touching By Others

No one should touch or hold your bird unless they are instructed in the proper manner. Trusted friends and adults in your home can sit in a circle on the floor so the bird may be passed from one to another. Before each is passed the bird, that person should speak reassuringly in a low coaxing voice that promises safety and pleasure. Each should speak softly saying "Up" and make soft eye contact. Explain to each of them how to pet a bird. The more informed gentle humans a bird is exposed to, the more likely he is to be a friendly bird who expects pleasure from strangers. He will willingly go to strangers if he has been socialized carefully in this manner. "Pass the bird" and the "peek-a-boo" games were first articulated by bird behaviorist Sally Blanchard.

Adolescence - A Time Of Transition

The first two years are critical. At about 18 months of age, the bird will begin pulling away somewhat. Be consistent and gentle with him at this time. Emotional separating is a natural milestone. He is no longer a baby and his relationship with you will change slightly. He may not be as accepting of the intimate full body caressing. Give him a little space but under no circumstances lessen your time or attention.

Some species are less interested in physical intimacy but all species should be offered the chance to enjoy the pleasure many birds get from such intimacy. Birds are individuals—some will enjoy more touching, some less.

This may last several months and he may be more interested in having you preen him.

Choose a group of nape feathers, get down to the skin level and gently pull a separate feather through your thumb and forefinger; go to the next feather and do the same thing.

If the bird has been lovingly and correctly managed, by the time he reaches 18 months of age, he will be a well-behaved, loving, confident, gentle companion for the rest of your life.

At this time, some birds begin to refuse to step up to come from the cage. A bird at this time should be offered the choice of coming from the cage on "Up" or being brought from the cage in a towel. This toweling should be done calmly, gently and in a matter-of-fact manner. Offered the choice, birds will choose to step up after a time or two of being brought from the cage in a towel. When a bird next refuses, show him the towel. You will find he will come out on Up, by his own choice, when shown the towel.

Don't feel rejected at his temporary change of attitude. In the wild he would be part of the juvenile flock, interacting and playing with his peers. This short period is analogous to the terrible twos one experiences with human children but isn't as bad as the awfulness of puberty in human children. It passes quickly and your loving relationship will resume, deepen, and become richer with experience and time.

You may think some of these suggestions are time-consuming, but your bird will likely outlive you and think what kind of life he would have if he were not a well-behaved, trusting, and accepting adult. A well-loved well-behaved companion bird will be a welcome member of any family. A bird is forever (almost) and he deserves the very best you and your breeder can offer. Make arrangements in your will for your bird. Most of the larger species can live 40-75+ years. A cockatiel has a natural life span of 25 years with good care and a good diet. Greys and macaws can live for 50-75 years, given regular health care and a nutritious varied diet. Some Amazons have lived past 100 years.

The most important way you can show your love is to allow your bird to be a parrot. He is not a perfect little robot who will respond in only one way to particular stimuli. Parrots are very complex animals with complex reasons why they behave as they do. If you are a perfectionist, you will have to concentrate this inclination in some other part of your life. Don't expect perfection or perfect behavior even if you behave perfectly toward the bird.

You may find that other methods work better for you and your bird. Whatever you choose to do, however, must be firmly based on a relationship of mutual trust, respect, and love. My advice is based on my experience, research, and a common sense approach. As Steve Martin (respected trainer and behaviorist) tells us: "The best approach is to never make the bird do anything it doesn't want to do, but find ways to use Positive Reinforcement to encourage the bird to do what you want him to do".

Don't allow problems or inappropriate behavior to accumulate or escalate. Don't hesitate to call your breeder, your avian vet, an avian behaviorist, or an experienced bird keeper regarding temporary or minor behavioral or health problems or for recommendations to professionals for your more serious concerns.

Life After Weaning - II

In part I, I concentrated on the socialization and behavioral aspects of getting to know your new bird. This article addresses many of the other areas that are important to your bird's well being and his interaction with you.

Foods

Continue to expose him to new foods, new tastes, new colors, new shapes. Don't allow him to get bored with the same old tastes day after day. Experiment: offer him a carrot stick or a piece of romaine lettuce when you make your salad for dinner. Allow him to share a piece of toast with you in the morning. Some birds like eggs. Since eggs can contain salmonella, they must be very well done if offered to the bird.

Eating is a social activity in a flock and your bird will enjoy his own dish at dinner. Yuck you say? You haven't lived until your bird walks through your spaghetti!

Don't give him his favorite treat day after day. Offer a nut meat (use human grade nuts, unsalted), a "different" color grape, a small apple cinnamon rice cake, a small piece of pizza. Only your imagination and the bird's acceptance limit treats.

Birds are messy with their food. In the wild this flinging, pitching, and dropping half-eaten food ensures the next generation of food trees or shrubs because the ground is littered with seeds awaiting their time in the sun. If you want stucco walls, feed your bird bananas. A well-enjoyed pomegranate will spot nearby objects a very attractive red. Forewarned is forearmed!

Toys

Rotate his toys so there will always be something new even if this "new toy" was a toy he had last month. Chewing is an important activity. Always have a couple of chewable, killable toys. He may also like to chew his perches. Using natural branches with the bark intact may be very attractive to him. Willow, although a soft wood, is much loved by birds. He can also be offered small willow twigs for a hand-held good chewing time. If he actually consumes the wood, naturally he can't have it. I have never had a bird actually ingest his toys but it is something to be watched for.

Perches

The most comfortable and affordable perch is a natural branch. The bird's nails should touch the branch but larger and smaller diameters on the same branch will give him foot exercise. A smooth unvarying perch is asking for foot and hip trouble. Replace perches as necessary. Naturally the branches must be a safe wood from a tree that has never been sprayed and must be scrubbed and disinfected.

Wing And Nail Clipping

I give Greys a very conservative wing trim—usually the first four flight feathers. Greys are heavy bodied birds and if they are clipped too severely, they can cause serious injury to the breast and/or sternum when fluttering down to the floor from the cage. With a very severe clip, a bird can actually rip his tail (the preacher's nose area) from his body with a clumsy landing. Please see Wingclipping and the African Grey in this publication.

Observe the bird carefully after the clipping. Sometimes I will have a particularly strong or skillful flier who flies further than

I want him to fly. My aim is 15 feet without altitude gain. This flight length will ensure that the bird has enough lift to land safely. If a bird flies more than 15 feet, clip one more flight feather off of each wing.

Some of the aerodynamic birds like the macaws, small conures, cockatiels may require a most severe clip for their safety in the home and to prevent escape. Clip the first five or six flights (nearest the tip of the wing). Brush aside the coverts and clip the flight so that the clipped portion of the shaft is above this last line of coverts. The stub is sandwiched between the outer wing coverts and the under wing coverts. This will ensure that the stub doesn't irritate or poke into the bird's flank. Of course, each feather must be checked to make sure you don't cut into a growing or blood feather. The coverts are the short overlapping feathers that cover the base of the flights and the tail feathers. Observe your bird for flight length and altitude and clip as many flights as are necessary.

Clipping a bird does not render the bird flightless. NEVER UNDER ANY CIRCUMSTANCES take your bird outside unless he is in a carrier or in a cage or in a harness.

I never clip the babies until they have learned to control their flight, land where they intended to land, and land on the floor safely. Often this means I am dodging several babies of several species "practicing" flying.

Once the babies learn they can really and truly fly, they tend to settle down and get on with the business of weaning. Losing weight during weaning is instinctive and unavoidable. Since flying is such an important activity, I have to clip the wings after several weeks and allow them to refocus on eating.

It is possible, using de-sensitizing methods, to train the bird to stand for toe nail clipping and wing clipping. If a bird's toenails are clipped a tiny bit weekly, the quick will recede and bleeding will seldom occur. This avoids pain for the bird and makes him more tractable during needed nail care.

After the bird becomes comfortable with and trusts the new owner, a nail file can be a good tool for beginning the de-sensitizing process. After the bird is comfortable with the new owner spreading his wings, it is possible to clip the wings without distressing the bird. It is critical that the bird be placed on a surface or substrate that is not slippery.

During this de-sensitizing period, be very careful and don't let anything untoward happen. The bird needs to believe that these exercises are harmless. Clipping the barest point off of a nail will not cause any pain or discomfort and will assure the bird that nail clipping is not to be feared.

As I mentioned in the socialization article, a very slow and careful routine will work best. The wing clipping exercise can begin with an examination of the scissors. Manipulate them, opening and closing them several times. Have them in the bird's sight for however long it takes for him to feel comfortable.

Begin the wing opening practice by slowly moving your hand from the back and top of the wings to the sides. Next begin running your thumb under the folded wing. Pay careful attention to his body language. After weeks or months, you should be able to spread his wing. Take as much time as you need. Never rush him. A cue—such as "Pretty wings."—is effective during this exercise.

Continue to do these exercises even when the bird doesn't need a toenail clip or a wing clip. It will keep the memory fresh for him and serve to remind him that neither form of grooming is to be feared.

Baths

I accustom the babies to their baths at first by spray bathing them when the flights and tails feathers emerge. Later when they are perching, I may hold them on my hand over the sink with their toes pinned firmly and scoop very warm water onto their backs and wings with my other hand. All the while reassuring them and telling them what fine brave birdies they are.

Some will enjoy playing in a stream of warm water from the faucet. Place something on the bottom of the sink so it isn't slippery. Some may enjoy a shallow bowl of very warm water. Others may prefer a misting while being held over the sink or perhaps

would be more receptive to a bath in or on the cage.

Many birds enjoy showering with their owners. There are PVC perches that attach by suction to the shower walls. Be gentle and reassuring while discovering the method your bird prefers.

If you take your bird into the bathroom when you are showering, the bird may well decide to join you. Many owners are successful by placing the bird on the shower curtain rod or on the top of the shower door or on the rim of the bathtub. You will want to put a towel over the surface for the bird to stand on.

Health

Weigh recently weaned birds daily. Adults may be weighed weekly. Keep a diary or calendar and record the weights. Weight loss is often the first indication that something may be wrong. A bird can hide most of the symptoms of illness but weight loss is one thing he cannot hide.

Pay attention to your bird's habits, check the poops daily, know how much water the bird drinks typically, how active he normally is. Minor changes, if continued, can indicate the need for a trip to your avian vet.

In all cases, have the blood calcium level checked every single year. Low blood calcium is life threatening. It can cause illness or even death if undiagnosed and untreated. Never give a calcium supplement to a companion bird unless directed to do so by an avian vet after a blood calcium level is run. Don't feed your bird a pellet with "extra" calcium. Companion birds don't need extra calcium, they need enough calcium.

Veterinarians

Take your bird to an avian vet. Be careful and informed regarding avian health and medicine if your vet doesn't see many birds. The values from the various tests will have significance to the avian vet, whereas the vet who sees few birds may not understand the significance or the relationship of one result to another. A vet who primarily sees cats, dogs, and other mammals may prescribe medicines that work very well on mammals but can cause serious liver and kidney damage in birds.

Avian research has made your baby healthier and will have a major influence on longevity. Support avian research and donate what you can to it on your baby's birthday. One facility that is doing much in the area of avian research is The University of Georgia, College of Veterinary Medicine, Athens, GA 30602-7371.

Other Pets

A bird should learn "Bad dog!" and/or "Bad cat!" when either of these animals approach his cage. Dog and cat bites or scratches, even if the skin is only broken, can result in death within days. If there is an encounter, take the bird to your avian vet **immediately** and explain the circumstances. The vet will prescribe an antibiotic, as the area of broken skin may be too small to be visualized. The bacteria associated with dog and cat teeth and claws are deadly to birds. No interaction between birds and other mammals should ever be encouraged or permitted.

Life After You

A bird is forever (almost) and he deserves the very best you and I can offer. Make arrangements in your will for your bird. Many birds have a human life span given regular health care and a nutritious varied diet.

The Adolescent Grey

Greys grow up. They don't stay docile accepting babies. Most importantly, they must be allowed to grow up. Think of your maturing Grey as a teenager. They can be rebellious. They may refuse to conform to formerly accepted standards of behavior. This is only a phase. It is not meant as rejection. A life and a being separate and apart from the parental figure is a hallmark of many maturing animals. You would accept this phase from a human teenager and try to live through the experience. As with a teenager, you have to be waiting on the other side and make the way back to you easy. You can lose a teenager's trust and confidence and you can lose a bird's trust and confidence. How you deal with the situation affects the outcome.

A maturing bird needs to express his autonomy. Within the core framework of "Up", "Down", no roaming, and no biting without a reason, allow a Grey freedom in all safe ways. It is important to concentrate at this time on the "core" behaviors. Areas outside of the core behaviors should be reserved for the bird, allowing him to make choices and decisions regarding his interaction or behavior.

Maturing birds should be given choices. If a maturing Grey is disciplined or corrected too much during this phase, he will resent it deeply. Some Greys become pluckers and biters at this stage, so understanding and proper actions are all important. Future problems can arise if a bird is forced into intimacy over which he has no control, if he is over-corrected and dominated at a time when he must separate emotionally, if he is not allowed autonomy, or if he is not allowed to become an adult.

All of the core behaviors should be enforced with patience, gentleness, persistence, consideration and, most important, an unemotional response to rebellion.

Practice avoidance of bad or unwanted behavior when a bird is maturing. Laddering, punishment, and isolation do not teach the bird anything except that he is a subservient being. This is not the way to establish a continuing relationship of trust and love with a maturing Grey.

I have not found that dominance and dominance-related issues play a significant role in the human/Grey relationship. Because of their sensitivity and intelligence, Greys need respect not dominance by their human companions.

A Grey is a bird with many of his ancient instincts intact. Confusion, anxiety, and resentment can occur when too many of these instincts are stifled. Domesticated animals with centuries and eons of association with humans behind them are much better prepared to deal with human dominance. A bird is not. He is, first and foremost, a wild animal. He is, for the most part, unknowable. His inner self is as hidden to us as the hearts of our fellow humans.

Your relationship with the bird will change, there is no doubt about it. He will be less accepting of scritches and long sessions on your chest. He will let you know when he wants these things. Most often this occurs at the end of the day, before bedtime. Don't force yourself on the bird. Establish an early understanding of the question "Do you want scratched?" Inquire of the maturing Grey before extended petting and quiet time—allow him to acquiesce or refuse. Empowerment makes a Grey strong emotionally and confident in himself and in humans who make this empowerment possible.

A Grey who has control over his life in the non-safety related areas is a bird who will remain willing to interact with humans. It would be wonderful if our Greys stayed the sweet compliant babies they are in the beginning, but this cannot be. We can have a satisfactory and fulfilling adult relationship, similar to the warm and satisfying relationship we have with our adult children. We can never forget the babyhood and the childhood and regret their passing, but baby humans and baby birds grow up. They become their own persons with their own likes and dislikes. It is up to us to accommodate adulthood; the bird cannot and will not return to babyhood.

Greys need freedom to make some of the decisions that affect their lives and their persons. This freedom for birds, like independence and self-reliance in humans, makes them confident and self-assured. A Grey will be better able to meet change and challenge if he has the experience and the knowledge that he is able to successfully manage some aspects of his life.

I'm an advocate of a gentle and understanding approach to maturity. Allow your bird the freedom to grow and develop within a wide but firm framework of boundaries.

It is important to avoid confrontation, any physical or aggressive action, and excessive correction. Distraction and avoidance are the best approaches to use with the maturing Grey.

The rebellious periods can vary with the individual bird. There is a minor testing period that occurs at around six months of age. This may be the age in the ancient past when complete food independence occurred and a baby bird was no longer dependent on the parents for life and food.

In the wild, flocks of juveniles go through certain maturing activities. These include perfecting their flying skills, aerial playing and chasing, forming early bonds with non-family members, establishing their status on the playgrounds of Africa, and withdrawal from the parental group. For the pet Grey, this period of time may form the basis for what we, at around 18 months of age, call the "terrible twos". Our companion Greys don't have the opportunity to do what their age-old instincts may call for them to do. Instead we will be observing substitute behaviors.

Activity and freedom will allow a Grey to develop in important ways. The independence-expressing stage is a risky stage. Understand and accept that it will come and it will go—in its own time and in its own manner.

Wingclipping And The African Grey

Clipping birds' wings is done mainly for their own safety. Birds can fly into windows, doors, ceiling fans, hot cooking foods, and any number of places in the home where they can injure themselves.

Wing clipping is also a protection against birds escaping into the out-of-doors. Once outside, an indoor flightless bird can easily take flight with the help of a gust of wind. Unfortunately, escaped birds have little chance of survival outdoors. They face death from a predator or starvation, while at home their owners grieve for their lost pet.

When clipping a bird's wings, it is **very important** that the clip be done properly and that the first wing clip is done only after a baby bird has learned to fly with precision and control.

The First Clip

An agile, confident, sure-footed Grey is the product of being allowed to fledge.

Allowing a baby bird to learn to fly enables him to develop coordination and control. He learns to land where he intends to land, learns how to flutter to the floor safely, and learns how to control his body. After he is clipped, this knowledge and confidence stays with him. A bird that knows how to control his body is much less likely to be injured.

If a Grey is clipped before he learns to fly with competence and control, he may not become a confident out-going bird. He may be fearful and insecure because he has not discovered his body's natural grace. This grace is learned through flight proficiency.

A baby Grey should be allowed to fully fledge. If the birds and the babies are clipped on an individual basis, taking into account their confidence level, strength, determination and power, this learned control and flying skill has become ingrained in the birds.

This baby has not been clipped yet. Allowing the babies to learn controlled flight is a must.

As a consequence, they are much less likely to land awkwardly when fluttering to the floor.

I let my babies fly until I can't stand it anymore, but I have a high tolerance for inconvenience.

The Importance Of A Proper Clip

There are two major areas of concern when doing a proper wing clipping; how many feathers to cut and where to cut the feathers. When done properly, a bird will be able to fly a short distance, control his flight, and be able to make a safe landing.

When a bird's wings are clipped incorrectly after he learns to fly, he may lose his confidence and the capability of controlling his body. He discovers, through pain and even injury, that what he previously learned about flying is no longer possible.

The primary flight feathers are the only feathers that should be clipped. Many clip birds' flight feathers at, or slightly below, the level of the upperwing coverts. With this method, the birds will be after the exposed ends of the shafts all the time and the shafts will become splintered from the constant grooming. The sharp, splintered ends seem to irritate their body and bother them psychologically. They are never satisfied with the ends of the shaft. How could they be? They can't groom the cut shortened feather into submission and order.

There is a physiological component as well as a psychological component when one considers how important flight feathers are to a bird's safety and life. A damaged feather reduces flight efficiency and interferes with escape. Birds appear to be quite concerned about these "half" feathers.

I recommend that the shaft be cut so that the cut end is sandwiched between the underwing coverts and the upperwing coverts. The flight is clipped just above the feather barbules; none of the barbules should be present on the cut shaft. These are a few reasons why:

•The cut edge isn't exposed to wear and doesn't get splintered and frayed. Since flight feathers are so important, the bird is concerned about the frayed end and will constantly try to smooth and groom it. The cut end is cushioned and doesn't dig into the bird's flank and irritate either the body or the mind.

•With a longer length of flight shaft, the bird is brought up short when he reaches the end of a long, sweeping grooming stroke. He is left with a feeling of incompleteness. He also can't "zip" up the half feather properly. This cut eliminates the problem.

•An additional benefit, albeit an unimportant one, is the clip reveals the lovely scallops of the upperwing coverts. The scalloped edge presents a very neat and pleasant appearance. No frayed, splintered shaft is showing; no frazzled, ragged feather barbules are showing. It is a very attractive clip.

• When I clip the babies and the birds, they

do "search" for the flights for a while, but this soon passes. It's almost like out of sight, out of mind. They don't get into the rhythm of the long sweeping grooming stroke only to be brought up short by an incomplete feather with a cut splintered end.

The cut end is protected, as it is between the upperwing covert and the underwing covert. I have never seen a splintered feather shaft with this clip, so I know the birds aren't chewing, grooming, or paying attention to the end as they did when I clipped the flight longer.

This clip is not a guarantee that a bird will never pluck. However, I believe a bird will be less inclined to pluck if he isn't constantly reminded that he is helpless to escape danger. I believe several half feathers and the resulting irritation, both mental and physical, produced by the cut and splintered ends will cause him to pay much more attention to his feathers and increase his feeling of helplessness. He can't know he is safe from predators, it's in the genes.

How To Clip

The flights of an African Grey should be clipped so that the cut end of the flight is sandwiched between the upper wing coverts (the short overlapping feathers that cover the base of the flights on the top of the wing) and the underwing coverts on the underside of the wing. If the cut edge is between these matching coverts, it won't poke into the bird's flank and possibly irritate him.

Towel the bird and place him on his back. Spread the wing. Carefully clip the flight from the underside of the wing so that the cut end is above the level of the coverts. Gently lift each flight feather and push away the coverts so that the coverts aren't accidentally clipped. Clip the flight at the point where the feather barbules begin on the shaft of the flight feather. There should be no barbules on the shaft of the cut flight feather.

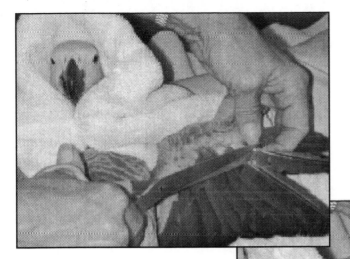

Watch carefully for blood feathers. Fortunately these are very obvious. A blood feather will be encased in a spongy sheath and will have black, brown or red coloring in the sheath. Mature sheaths are hollow and quite hard.

Greys need to be custom cut.
Each bird is different in strength and determination. I suggest that four feathers be clipped initially. Watch the bird to see how far he can fly or flutter with four flights clipped. If he is able to fly or flutter more than 15 feet, clip one more feather from each wing. Observe him again for distance and altitude. If he can flutter more than 15 feet, clip one more flight feather on each wing. Observe him again for distance and altitude. The 15-foot downward flight path will enable the bird to flutter safely to the floor with control and adequate power.

When a Grey has molted for the first time, don't clip the same number of flights that were clipped when he was a baby. The babies are strong from exercise and determined because flight is so important for survival. They don't know they are safe but are driven to learn to fly by ancient instincts. A bird that has been clipped for months has not gotten the exercise and is not as driven to fly as the babies are. Consequently, fewer

flights may be clipped for his safety indoors. Begin at the beginning—with four flight feathers and custom clip for a 15-foot downward glide path. You will find that fewer flights need to be clipped for an older Grey than for a baby Grey.

Do not clip only one wing as this will result in a significant loss of control and interfere with landing accuracy and balance. Do not leave the last flight feathers (at the leading edge of the wing) uncut for appearances sake. The flights usually left unclipped with this "convict" clip are numbers 9 and

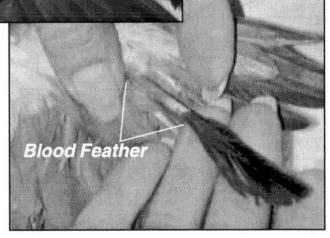

Notice the large swollen shaft. Gently pinch the shaft (starting at the end of the flight farthest from the body) to make sure the shaft is hard and mature. The portion of the flight feather where the shaft is __HARD__ and mature can be clipped to avoid breaking during vigorous play or from an awkward landing. __NEVER__ cut the soft swollen blood-filled portion of the living blood feather.

10. This clip is called the "convict" clip because it allows a bird to escape. These unclipped leading edge flights are also vulnerable to injury and breaking, as they have no support from adjacent feathers.

Stress In African Greys And Other Birds

Stress can cause major behavioral problems with any bird, but it is of even more concern with African Greys. Greys are sensitive to the moods of humans and the ambiance of the human environment because they are genetically vulnerable. The habitat where they evolved is, for the most part, on the margins of forested areas. We often see Greys foraging on the ground in nature films. Surely birds that are ground foragers must be more alert to danger and more aware of what is behind and around them. It **pays** in terms of staying alive to be aware of their surroundings and to be sensitive to the watching eyes of a predator.

Jean Pattison, the African Queen, made a quite original observation that supports this. African Greys produce larger clutches (three, four, or five eggs) than many other species of large parrots. If all these eggs hatched and the babies lived to adulthood, Africa would soon be covered in African Greys. In nature, species with a high death rate produce many more young than those which have fewer predators and a lower death rate. Might it mean that predation and a high death rate in Greys require larger clutches to ensure the survival of the next generation?

Parrots are prey animals. The unique responses by prey animals to outside stimuli are very different than the responses of predators such as humans, dogs or cats. Being part time ground feeders, Greys are even more at risk than many other species of birds. It is almost impossible for humans, as predators, to understand the stresses that prey animals experience. Actions by a pet owner, which are similar to those of a predator in the wild, can unintentionally trigger high levels of stress in a bird.

The characteristics that make Greys such superb companion animals also make them vulnerable to self-destructive behavior in the face of high stress—from fear, threat, illness, uncertainty, abandonment, or anxiety.

Greys are not like dogs or horses or other domestic animals that accept the dominance of humans. Human attempts to dominate them only lead to stress in Greys. Punishing a Grey is not only useless, but can cause psychic trauma of immense proportions. A Grey does not have the cognitive ability to relate punishment to his behavior. Instead he regards punishment as abuse, the punisher as the abuser, and his environment as a horror-filled world.

A loved one's illness or death, an unhappy or disintegrating marriage, physical violence, drugs or alcohol abuse, environmental insecurity, fear associated with other companion animals, a disliked human, unkind handling by a vet or groomer or other stressful events may trigger plucking, phobia, or aberrant behavior in our sensitive and empathetic Greys.

Layne Dicker uses a great visual aid in his lectures relating to stress. He draws an imaginary line below which an individual bird is able to deal with the inevitable stress associated with captivity and living with humans. If a bird's current stress level is near this boundary, the addition of just one more stressful event or act puts the bird above that line and triggers unnatural behavior.

If a bird is suddenly exhibiting stressful behavior, it is natural for an owner to think that the most recent event or act is the cause and to attempt to deal with that one event. However, fear, phobia, biting, or other aberrant behavior in Greys is most likely the result of a stressful environment that has finally crossed over the line described by Layne. It is important to examine a bird's entire environment, looking for multiple sources of stress, and eliminate as many as possible.

The intelligent and sensitive Grey reacts more positively and more appropriately to the human as teacher, guide, parental figure, mentor, and caregiver.

If there is any human science/art application to the management of birds, it lies in child psychology. The similarities are striking. We see, in modern society, what the results of inadequate and uninformed child rearing accomplishes. We can see in our birds what inappropriate, heavy handed, and misapplied management techniques do to our birds.

Greys are not aggressive birds. They are taught to be aggressive by humans. They bite because they remember mistreatment. Those memories may include:

• Lack of respect.

• Lack of consideration of their desires.

• Aggressive human actions or physical pain.

• Intimidation.

• Domineering humans.

• Sensory deprivation as punishment.

A Grey needs to have his person and his space respected. We are all familiar with humans who "invade" our personal space, who touch us without our consent. A Grey may be eating or playing or taking a nap when his human wants to interact. His desires should be considered. An early understanding of "Do you want to come to me?" or a similar phrase, gives him an option and serves to assure one that interaction or touching is welcome.

What needs to change is the way we think and feel about the things our birds do. We are the ones who need to adjust to living with birds. We need to accept that they are from another world—a world we have a great deal of difficulty understanding.

If a bird steps up and down; if a bird doesn't bite us without a reason; if a bird doesn't roam—these are the behaviors we need to enforce for their own safety. If they love and trust us; permit us to interact, pet and kiss them—that is a product of the way we feel and behave towards them. We have to be the unselfish giving partner in the relationship. If we are, they will love and trust us. That is the highest degree of intimacy. We have animals in our homes that, for the most part, are first generation from the jungles of Africa. That they love and trust us is a testimony to our adjustment to them—not theirs to us.

Do all you can to keep the level of stress as low as possible. Be kind, gentle, and patient with your Grey. Do not contribute to his stress load by attempts to dominate or punish or change his parrotness. Accept that he is a bird—not one of the more familiar domestic animals we have dealt with and trained and punished into good or acceptable behavior for so long.

There are many things a pet owner can do to minimize stress in the environment. Please see <u>Managing Stress in African Grey Parrots</u> which contains a number of suggestions for reducing stress.

Managing Stress
In African Grey Parrots

Many of the behavior problems seen in Greys result from not permitting the bird to be a bird or from a failure to understand and accept that Greys are prey animals from a wild world beyond our knowing and have little in common with familiar domesticated animals.

Greys are exotic beings from a strange land. They don't understand our customs or our language. It is up to us, as guardians of a treasure, to treat them with the same care and courtesy one would offer a well-loved and welcome human visitor in our homes. We should be grateful they love and trust us; that they care enough about us to want to communicate with us in our own language; that they permit us to love them. We should rejoice when their wild instincts are overcome by the love they feel for us.

I have observed wild caught Greys in a pair or breeding situation and find that they are not aggressive. They do feel fear (justified) when the presence of humans intrudes. However, when closed circuit cameras are used to observe them, the birds fail to show aggression. They play, give and take food from one another, groom, and interact with each other in a non-aggressive manner. Aggressive behavior is, however, seen in breeding Greys who have been companion birds. Companion Greys, domestic and imported, are taught to be aggressive by humans.

Some reasons for aggression in companion Greys may be:

• Lack of respect for their desires in non-safety related behavior or respect for their persons.

• Lack of consideration or compassion for their captive and utterly dependent status.

• Aggressive human actions or physical pain. Pushing, shoving, chasing, or shaking a clipped bird is frightening and dangerous to that bird. Flicking the beak, dropping the bird to the floor, or striking the bird anywhere on his body are completely foreign acts to an avian species to whom pain and aggression mean death is close.

• Intimidation. Standing over a Grey, glaring, or staring to intimidate him impacts the sense of confidence and comfort which he needs in order to love and trust his human caregiver.

• Domineering humans. A Grey, like other helpless and dependent beings, will be unable to trust humans who are critical and punishing and who wish to micro-manage natural actions.

• Sensory deprivation as punishment. Would we place a child who misbehaves in a punishment situation involving sensory deprivation in an attempt to change behavior? Would that child love and trust us? Or would that child come to view us as a controlling and implacable being?

Birds are wild animals and comparing them to domesticated animals fails—in behavior, in intelligence and in most other ways. Trying to compare birds (prey animals) to predators, such as cats and dogs, is also invalid. Eradication of a bird's genetic inheritance of prey behaviors will require thousands of generations of selective breeding, if such an eradication is possible.

There are many things that can cause stress in birds. If the stress level becomes too high, a bird can begin biting, self mutilate, pluck, or become phobic. Never try to dominate or punish a Grey. As one learns about birds and their natural activities, it becomes clear why these actions are stressful and should be avoided. You will only succeed in creating stress in the bird and losing your pet's trust.

Intelligent and sensitive Greys suffer most when these punishing and control oriented approaches are used by human caregivers. They respond more positively and more appropriately to a human as teacher, guide, parental figure, mentor, and caregiver. Positive reinforcement, encouragement, respect, and a compassionate view of dependence works to shape behavior—in human children, in dogs, in horses......and in birds.

Domination

Some domesticated animals naturally strive for dominance. However, Greys are dramatically different. This fact must be taken into account when attempting to apply management techniques used on dogs and horses to the world of birds. Domesticated animals, for the most part, wish to please humans. A bird wishes to please himself.

A Grey does not strive for dominance. Why should he? He sees himself, for the most part, as an equal who should be treated with courtesy, respect, and allowed to live his life within a narrow range of acceptable behavior. The behaviors, I believe, that need be enforced in a Grey are "Up" and "Down", no roaming and no

biting without a reason. Beyond these, a bird should be allowed to be a bird, so long as his safety and health are not compromised. These guidelines are similar to things a child must learn if he is to grow to an adult, such as "Don't play in the streets.", "Don't go off with strangers.", "Look both ways before you cross the street.", etc.

Micro-managing a bird's life, as with a human child, creates resentment and smothers independence, self-confidence, and self-reliance. Human attempts to dominate them lead to stress in Greys. Unlike dogs or horses, Greys will not accept the dominance of humans. I find the application of "pack" words to the description of the management of Greys distressing. Words like alpha, leader of the flock and dominance really have no place in the techniques used to manage a flock animal like a Grey. The attempt to establish ourselves as "leader", "alpha", or "dominant" in a nonexistent flock hierarchy is counter to the instincts which drive our non-domesticated wild Greys. These attempts, I believe, create stress and are the root of many of the behavior and health problems that we see in so many Greys.

Punishment

Punishment is very stress producing. Punished Greys learn, through fear, intimidation, isolation, physical and psychological pain, what can happen to them. The lack of comprehensive understanding by a wild animal, whose reality does not include the concept of punishment, is the real horror. The apparent randomness of the punishment, given the lack of cognitive understanding and reasoning and the instinctive rejection of punishment as a disciplinary tool, can cause psychic trauma of immense proportions. Aggression and physical pain mean death to the fragile body of a bird. That a bird does know. Fear biting can become habitual biting—a way for the bird to avoid the aggressive human acts which appear to be random and inappropriate in response to some instinctual behavior. The rebellion associated with coming of age triggers inappropriate responses in humans who fail to understand and appreciate that birds change as they mature. Roaming and exploration are important to young birds and are not done to trigger annoyance in humans. Vocalizing is the instinctive way to keep in contact with the flock. Vocalizing and calling is a way for a bird to reassure himself he is not alone and vulnerable.

Any apparent docility by a Grey in the aftermath of punishment is more likely a numb acceptance of apparently random and seemingly unavoidable punishment—acceptance without real understanding, coupled with fear, avoidance, and resentment directed at the punishing human.

Striking a bird, dropping a bird to the floor, isolation in a small cage or carrier in a remote location, placing the bird in a bath tub or other inappropriate place as punishment, covering the cage as punishment, laddering, intimidation through staring or glaring are some worthless and counterproductive acts of punishment.

There are few ways to punish a Grey. Their physical fragility and emotional sensitivity preclude almost all types of punishment. Their psyches reject it. In any case, it doesn't work—not in the long run. The bird knows who is punishing him; he just doesn't understand why. But he will remember and not forgive the punisher.

Overhead Movement

The unique responses to outside stimuli

by prey animals are very different than the responses of a predator. Staring, glaring, physical aggression, and overhead movement are perceived as dangerous and life threatening. Even captive raised Greys will duck when a dark shape passes over. Don't leave a bird outdoors on a porch or near a window where large birds can fly by and frighten him. Avoid standing over or hovering over a Grey in a threatening manner in an effort to intimidate him.

Flight Mechanism

The flight mechanism of a prey animal like a Grey is well developed—and must be for survival. The knowledge of the fragility of their bodies is in the genes. A clipped bird cannot fly away from a perceived danger or threat.......and our Greys must be clipped for their own safety in a human environment with its accompanying dangers and perils. This increases the stress level when a bird thinks he is being threatened.

Striking or Hitting

Striking a bird anywhere on his body, snatching a bird up roughly or bodily, shouting, an aggressive stance or movement, are frightening to birds. Their bones are much more fragile than the bones of mammals and they can easily be injured. They are built for flight, not fight with their hollow bones and other physical evolved adaptations for weight reduction.

Staring and Glaring

Glaring at a Grey in an attempt to intimidate him calls up the ancient self. It is no coincidence that frightened, abused, or phobic birds should not be looked at straight on or stared at. Sideways looks are much less threatening. The full-on stare or glare is the predator's intense look at his dinner. A Grey finds staring or glaring indicative of the close attention paid by the predator to his chosen target. Staring and glaring are threatening and intimidating.

Laddering

Laddering a Grey, as punishment or behavior modification, in an unfamiliar area by a domineering human is an anxiety producing event. This kind of attempt to reinforce the mistaken notion that a Grey is a subservient being is long remembered and much resented. Permanent cessation of this futile exercise can, over time, diminish the anxiety and the resentment generated by this attempt at domination.

Isolation

Any bird will be quiet when isolated or when faced with sensory deprivation from being placed alone in a dark room or having the cage covered as punishment or to correct unwanted behavior. For a prey animal that is dependent on his senses for life itself, this can be a devastating punishment. Putting a Grey in an empty bath tub or shower stall alone is an abhorrent act that will not be forgotten soon.

Punishing a bird with isolation doesn't work. The bird may be quiet after he is isolated due to sensory deprivation. However, this doesn't curb or stop the screaming or noise or biting or whatever behavior caused the isolation. He doesn't make the connection between isolation and/or sensory deprivation and the behavior that causes it. A bird is not able to reason out cause and effect. If he knew what acts, instincts or behavior would cause isolation, he wouldn't do them.

A Grey is thought to be comparable to a two-five year old human emotionally and mentally. Would you isolate a child this age to punish him or to modify his behavior?

Wing Clipping

The repeated removal of deeply seated flight feathers in the aftermath of broken blood feathers can lead to a fearful or phobic Grey. A proper wing clipping is paramount to ensure that Greys can control their bodies when they flutter to the floor. A controlled landing by a Grey who has fledged fully prior to clipping will prevent injury. Please read the article Wingclipping and The African Grey for my recommendation for clipping.

If a blood flight feather is injured, do all you can to avoid pulling it. Consult with your avian vet for recommended techniques to deal with an injured blood feather before the bird breaks one. Some of the recommendations may be: stopping the bleeding and gluing the break closed; packing the break with a paste of cornstarch and Aloe Vera Gel; pressure to stop the bleeding. Clipping the feather off where the shaft is mature and hard will help avoid further injury to the flight. Do not use a Quik Stop type product on a bleeding or broken blood feather. There is the danger of systemic toxicity. A paste of cornstarch and Aloe Vera Gel is much safer. Aloe is a soothing substance for wounds. It should be a part of an emergency first aid kit and should be refrigerated after opening.

If the feather must be removed, have it done at your avian vet's office. Greys can and may become fearful of the owner for the great pain inflicted when a flight is pulled. The pain, the necessary restraint, and the fear or panic of the owner at the bleeding can cause stress for the bird.

Clipping Nails

The use of one of the cement perches may lessen the stress associated with clipping the toenails. These perches reduce but do not eliminate the need for grooming the nails. The early introduction of a ceramic nail file or one of the nail files designed for use with artificial nails may further reduce the need for toenail clipping. If a bird or baby can be brought, patiently and gently, to accept the owner filing his nails, this may further reduce the need for grooming and the stress associated with restraint. If the sharp ends of the nails are clipped regularly, without pain or discomfort, the bird will be accepting of grooming without restraint, thus lessening stress from toweling.

One of the more unfortunate signs of stress is feather destruction or self-mutilation. When a Grey discovers that plucking or mutilation relieve his inner anxieties, it can become habit forming unless immediate measures are taken to interrupt the bond that begins to form between temporary relief and habituation. A complete and thorough examination to rule out a physical or medical cause is a necessary first step.

The use of drugs and collars for plucking is always distressing, for the bird and for the owner. Birds who mutilate their bodies, however, may require one or both to save their lives. The precipitating events are sometimes obscure; the resolution, if possible, is time consuming and painful for all involved. Some drugs work with some humans, some don't. Sometimes humans are prescribed one drug after another until the one that is best for them is discovered. This type of investigation may be necessary for a bird, too, if it has been determined that a drug is necessary to save his life.

Since mutilation may have the same mental root in birds as in people, drugs may work. It is clear that some mental distress affects self-mutilators who have no medical or physical cause for this behavior. Mutilating is a life-destroying act.

Any drug or calming herb or other preparation should only be administered at the direction of, and under the supervision of an avian vet. Careful and constant observation is necessary by the owner to avoid the sometimes serious adverse reactions. Do not medicate a bird for feather destruction or mutilation without consulting with an avian vet.

One of the coming of age behaviors that many pet owners find difficult to deal with is when the bird refuses to come from the cage on the "Up" request. Offering the bird a choice of coming from the cage on the "Up" request or coming from the cage in a towel has been a successful way to deal with this temporary situation. It is similar to offering a child the choice of taking his bath at 6pm or 8pm. He still has to take his bath but has control of when. Empowerment and choices make birds, and children, strong emotionally and self-confident.

Taking the bird from the cage in a towel must be done gently, unemotionally, with regret, without anxiety, without haste. The bird will choose to step up after a time or two of coming from the cage in a towel. Using a bath towel folded in half, place each hand on the underside of the towel for protection and gently envelop the bird in the towel. Do not compress the breast when removing him from the cage. Grasp him gently around the body from the sides. Keep the towel near the cage. Don't use a towel that is customarily used for grooming—have a special towel. Scolding the towel after removing it from the bird's body can be effective. Gently place the bird on the cage top or play gym. Do not let him fall. Make sure he is securely perching. Remove the towel gently from around his body and then scold the towel.

The next time the bird refuses to step up to come from the cage, show him the towel and ask, "Do you want the towel?" Give him the choice of the towel or coming out on "Up".

Birds who roam may need to be returned to the cage thousands of times until they learn they are not to roam. The only exception that I recommend is when the bird is coming directly to you. If there are any side trips, he should be returned immediately to the cage or play area. This needs to be done consistently—every single time the bird leaves the cage. If caught in the act of leaving the cage, he can be told, "Hey, get back on the cage." It may take a number of times until he understands this phrase, but eventually he will understand. He may not comply but he will understand. Roaming and exploration are important to young birds. These are natural and normal acts. A bird that is not familiar with his environment is lunch in the wild.

Birds sometimes are noisy when their humans are trying to watch TV. They are often competing with the TV for attention. A bird will be less noisy when quiet is desired if he is provided with a time-consuming treat or given a new toy or favorite toy that is reserved for this type of occasion. Being placed on the cage top or a play area instead of being locked in the cage will also lessen the noise. Soft contact calls and frequent eye contact will reassure him he isn't ignored or alone. A flock animal feels vulnerable when he is alone. Companionship and flock interaction is vital for survival in the wild set-

ting and these traits do not change in our companion birds.

My experience is with my own pets and my own baby Greys. I don't have these kinds of behavior problems reported in my own babies. I think this is because I have convinced and educated buyers of my birds that the methods so often used by others aren't required. In fact, they are counter-productive if they want to keep the same sweet, tame bird I sold to them.

We need to understand our Greys. Ignore or divert their attention when they are exhibiting what we may perceive as annoying behaviors, as long as these natural or normal behaviors are unrelated to safety issues such as Up and Down, no roaming, and no biting without a reason.

Biting is a result of not paying attention to the bird's body language or a reaction to a dominating or threatening stance or act. Biting can become habitual from use of aggressive techniques which threaten or frighten the bird. Tame birds that are laddered as punishment bite more, not less. The owners who have stopped using aggressive and counter-productive techniques report a change for the better in their Greys. I hope through these articles to change the mindset of the controlling humans who want to micro-manage the lives of these wonderful creatures and transform their Greys into nice little robots who don't bite or scream or annoy or pluck or roam.

The Facts About Punishment

By Bobbi Brinker and S. G. Friedman, Ph.D.

Nowadays, the issue of punishment has become an emotional minefield of misconceptions, good intentions, and general confusion. And this is the good news. We would be loath to return to a time when the use of punishment was unquestioned and was the most common, if not sole, strategy for changing undesirable behavior. A large part of the present confusion results from the perennial gap between research and practice. However, the negative effects of some forms of punishment have been studied scientifically and are well documented. These studies reveal compelling information about the detriments of punishment that no parrot guardian should be without.

Our pets do not understand complex interpersonal humanisms such as rage, retribution or retaliation.

Another problem is that punishment is what most of us do best ... or at least first. It is our teaching legacy passed down from generation to generation. We are virtually surrounded by punishing strategies used to influence our behavior: From overdue library books to dogs without licenses; fines, penalties and reprimands whirl around us like leaves in a storm. For many of us, to give up punishment as our primary tool with which to influence negative behavior is to leave us empty handed. With this article, we hope to narrow the gap between the research and practice of punishment as it applies to companion parrots and provide the relevant information you need to base your choice of teaching strategies on facts rather than cultural inheritance.

A Functional Definition

It is often repeated that parrots don't respond to punishment. This misconception results from using the term too loosely in ways that describe the upset emotional state of the person delivering the punishment rather than its result on the bird's behavior. It is true that parrots do not respond to rage, retribution or retaliation. Although these negative consequences may be punishing to some of us, our pets will not understand such complex inter-personal humanisms. A clear, functional definition of punishment is needed to correct common misconceptions and enable us to measure the efficacy of our teaching strategies. From this perspective, science provides a more useful definition than Webster does: Simply and precisely, punishment is a consequence delivered after a behavior that serves to reduce the frequency or intensity with which the behavior is exhibited.

There are two very important points to make about this definition: First, the effectiveness of any particular punishment is a highly individual matter The proof of effectiveness is in the resulting behavior. A consequence that is punishing to one individual (i.e., that reduces a behavior) may actually be reinforcing (i.e., maintains or increases a behavior) to a different individual. Therefore, we can make an informed guess about what may be an effective punishment, but we can't know for sure until we see what happens to the frequency of the behavior it follows. Shouting at a screaming bird is a good example of a consequence that is intended to be a punishment, but, as evidenced by the increased screaming of many birds, it is often a very effective reward.

This brings us to the second point needing clarification: Punishment is not one single strategy but a collection of strategies that exist on a continuum from very mild to highly aversive approaches. Given our definition of punishment as a behavior-reducing technique, it is important to understand the nature of this continuum because there are some strategies on the very mild end that can be conditionally recommended with certain birds or for certain behaviors.

Strategies for Reducing Behavior

One mild form of punishment is to withdraw or remove something desirable, such as our hand or shoulder for perching. Many people have successfully reduced their bird's "beaky" behavior with this strategy, including watchband nibbling, earring snatching and shirt button cracking. Each and every time the bird engages in such behaviors, immediately but calmly and gently set him down for just a few seconds, then cheerfully offer him another opportunity to perch on your hand. With just a few repeated trials, most birds make the connection between the offensive behavior and being set down and they choose to stay put on your terms. No anger, frustration or rough handling is needed; only immediacy, removal, and a subsequent opportunity to do it right.

Removing a bird from your hand for beaky behavior is also a good example of how the effectiveness of a particular strategy varies from individual to individual. Some birds do not want to be handled. For them, the consequence of being set down would be reinforcing as evidenced by their continued or increased beaky behaviors.

Another example of mild punishment is to ignore a particular behavior, meaning to withhold attention for a behavior that has been previously given attention. Ignoring is not as easy as it sounds, but it is very effective when matched to the appropriate behavior and executed well. Here's the critical scientific fact about ignoring that you need to know: The first reaction most birds have to being ignored is to increase the frequency or intensity of the negative behavior. If your nerves wear thin and you stop ignoring during this predictable but temporary burst of behavior, you will reinforce it at this new higher frequency or intensity! Alternatively, if you maintain stalwart ignoring and do not waver, the behavior will eventually decrease.

Ignoring problem behavior is only effective for those behaviors that are being maintained because of our attention and for those behaviors that can be completely and totally ignored. Some behaviors cannot or should not be ignored. Biting is a case in point. Although it is often recommended that to reduce biting, one should simply buck up and ignore it, this is not a practical strategy.

Minimizing one's reaction is certainly a good idea but it is darn near impossible to maintain the composure of a stone while being pinched with the vice-like beak of the average parrot. Also, it is likely that many birds find the tactile sensations associated with biting inherently reinforcing, quite aside from our reactions. Indeed the only reliable way to teach a parrot not to bite is to not give him the opportunity to do so in the first place. Of course, self-injurious or otherwise dangerous behaviors need to be dealt with using strategies other than ignoring, as well.

When using mild punishment, ensure that the ratio of positive interactions to negative interaction is high. In an environment rich with praise and attention, mild methods to reduce behavior such as ignoring can be effective without apparent negative side effects. Nonetheless, not all of us are good ignorers or can ignore all types of behavior. And, some people find it too difficult to use the removal/withdrawal strategy with absolute consistency Know your personal limitations and

choose your teaching strategies to ensure success.

At the other end of the punishment continuum is the presentation or delivery of aversive consequences. Unfortunately, the list of examples of this form of punishment is long and too familiar. Aversive punishment includes consequences such as shaking your hand to unseat a bird's balance, squirting water at a bird from a spray bottle, throwing things at a bird or his cage, dropping a bird on the floor, shutting a bird in a closet, covering a bird for extended periods during nonsleep time, knocking a bird off his perch, forcing a bird to rapidly and repeatedly step from one hand to another, blowing in a birds face, shouting, hitting, and plucking out feathers.

Some people argue for the use of aversive punishment on the basis of its effectiveness; however, serious problems are likely to arise from the use of aversive strategies even in cases of short-term or narrowly defined success. For reasons explained below, no form of punishment that includes the presentation of aversive consequences should be used with companion parrots at anytime ... ever. It is not only unnecessary but also harmful. If you apply only one fact about punishment to teaching your parrot, let this be the one.

Problems With Mild Punishment

The use of even mild forms of punishment warrants careful deliberation and thoughtful planning. First, you should consider the nature of the behavior you hope to teach your bird to exhibit less often. It is not reasonable to try to eliminate natural behaviors such as the infamous cockatoo dawn greeting ceremony, those frustrating food-tossing marathon events or the hungry shark transformation that otherwise sweet birds exhibit when you dare to put your hand in their cages. With a little creativity, the responsibility for accommodating frustrating or annoying natural behaviors rests quite comfortably on human shoulders. Perhaps you can take your shower while your bird welcomes the day; special cups and cage aprons go a long way to reduce the mess caused by natural food- tossing behavior; and feathered sharks can be peaceably removed from their cages on perching sticks and returned to their feathered angel states once they are outside of their cages.

Second, carefully consider the probable cause of the problem behavior: Very often, the behavior driving you crazy is a legitimate expression of unmet needs. When this happens, the appropriate strategy is to meet the bird's needs rather than treating the communication as a problem behavior. For example, birds do not typically scream incessantly when they are well nourished, appropriately housed, provided ample time out of their cages, engaged in independent play, and offered daily, focused time with family members.

Finally, consider how to change the behavior. If there is a positive alternative strategy to even mild punishment (and in our experience there most often is), use it. Positive teaching strategies have all sorts of positive spin-offs and none of the detriments of punishment. Positives spin-offs for your bird include the opportunity to learn to do something more not less, to learn new behaviors rather than unlearn old ones, to live in an environment saturated with praise, and to increase confi-

dence that only good things happen in the presence of humans - a requisite for trust, There are many highly effective alternatives to punishment. Teaching acceptable replacement behaviors or teaching behaviors that are incompatible with the negative behavior are two examples well worth learning about.

In short, we suggest that you answer the following three questions before using mild punishment with your parrot: (1) Is it unreasonable or inappropriate to expect a bird to stop behaving in this way? (2) Is the negative behavior a result of an unmet need? (3) Is there a positive teaching strategy that can be used instead of punishment? If the answer to any of these questions is yes, look for ways to change your expectations, meet your bird's needs, and/ or use a positive teaching strategy to help you and your bird become the best possible companions for the long-run.

Unacceptable Side Effects of Aversive Punishment

Research on the effects of aversive punishment is not new nor has it been narrowly investigated. On the contrary, this research spans many decades and has been replicated with many different species of animals, including humans. Although there is some variability in the way researchers describe their results, the fact is there is a pattern of negative reactions or "side effects" that are consistently observed in many subjects who have been punished with aversive consequences.

The first predictable side effect is a sustained effort to escape the punishing situation. If escape is blocked, as with our caged and clipped companion parrots, the animal may (1) withdraw from further interaction, (2) suppress responding, (3) escalate or counter aggression, and/or (4) over-generalize fear, often to the point of phobia.

For most of us, these side effects are painful to read about no less observe, in our beloved parrots. Sadly, many of us have known or heard about birds that have withdrawn by refusing opportunities to come out of their cages. These poor souls cower dismally in the corners of their cages for hours on end. Other birds may suppress responding to the most basic activities. They can refuse to step up or even stop eating. It is not unheard of for birds to attack their owners or become fearful of people and things that never caused them any direct harm.

Based on these scientific facts, there is no justification for using aversive punishment with our birds. There are no long-term benefits, and the costs are grave. Ironically, it is the short-term effect of punishment that keeps so many of us using it. Every time an animal responds to punishment by doing something less often, the person who delivered the punishment is rewarded. For example, if your parrot stops chewing the windowsill when you throw a shoe at him, chances are you will throw shoes more often. This presents a significant obstacle to reducing our use of punishment to influence behavior and is worthy of introspection.

The commitment to change whatever we call ourselves in reference to our parrots, be it pet owner, caretaker, parent or guardian, we are all teachers in the most fundamental sense. Each and every moment spent with our birds is a moment that teaches them something about living with humans. In the perpetual role of teacher, we should borrow the physicians' guiding principle: First do no harm. We have learned from years of empirical study over hundreds of scientific experiments that in fact aversive punishment does do harm. We have also learned that even mild forms of punishment should be used cautiously and knowledgeably.

The individual nature, age, species and history of any particular bird add another level of complexity to choosing the best practices for our parrots. Some birds, those that are confident, bold and trusting, can be resilient to some punishment techniques. In other words, we may well get away with lesser teaching strategies with some birds under some conditions that would be detrimental to others. However, experience has shown that very young birds, re-homed birds, and birds with existing medical and/or behavioral problems are especially vulnerable to the adverse responses associated with punishment.

There will always be many unknowns about behavior; there will always be important variables that are out of our control. Behavior is just too complex for simplistic cookbook approaches to mentoring our birds where we look up problem behaviors in a table of contents and follow behavioral recipes. Each situation is unique and requires careful analysis and informed consideration. Facilitating well-adjusted, independent, confident companion parrots through the use of positive teaching techniques is more than just a commitment to learning new strategies; it is also a commitment to changing our legacy. The time for such change is now.

Hazards and Care of Your Bird

Teflon

No product that has Teflon or any non-stick coating belongs in a house with a bird. Teflon, and any non-stick coating, is very serious business for birds. Non-stick coatings are everywhere—space heaters, irons, bread machines, ovens and racks, ironing board covers, waffle irons, burner pans or grilles, etc. Be sure that any product you apply heat to does not have a non-stick coating. Open a window and run the range fan on high when you cook in case there is a non-stick coating on the grilles.

Some oven and oven components are coated with a shipping resin that can be fatal to a bird. Cook stove grilles can be heated to a high temperature in an outdoor grille to make sure there is no resin on them. It doesn't matter how careful you will be so that food doesn't burn; it doesn't matter if food sticks in aluminum or stainless steel pots and pans; it doesn't matter what the exact temperature is that non-stick coatings kill; it just doesn't matter. For the sake of the life of your bird: Do not use any product or buy any item that has a non-stick coating.

Self-Cleaning Ovens

Don't run the self-cleaning cycle with your birds in the house. If you have a new oven, run the self-cleaning cycle several times (with the racks in the oven) after removing your birds from the house. The high temperature generated by the self-cleaning feature will burn away the shipping resin if one is present. If you have not used the self cleaning feature in an existing oven, run it several times (with the racks in the oven) after removing your birds from the house to make sure that all the shipping resin, if one is present, is burned away.

Pick a summer day and take the bird from the house to use the self-cleaning feature if you need to use it or want to use it in the future. The stench from the shipping resin on the oven interior in the self cleaning mode in my new home was enough to drive us from the house. I can well believe it would have killed my birds had they been in the house.

A coating, meant to be burned away during use, on ceramic stovetop surfaces has been implicated in the deaths of birds. Take precautions, open windows, run the stovetop fan on high and keep your birds out of the kitchen, during the early weeks and months if you have a ceramic cooking surface. Will this save your bird? I don't know. An attempt to burn off the coating before the bird is present will certainly help.

Toxic Foods, Plants, Chemicals and Toy Safety

There are many substances—foods, plants and chemicals—that can cause injury and death to our birds. Birds have also been injured and even died from poorly made toys and cages. Of equal danger are electrical cords and outlets. Childproof your outlets and restrict roaming. Please read some of the articles below to learn more about protecting your bird. *(URLs for these articles are found in the Recommended Reading List in this publication)*

A - Zinc of Zinc Poisoning

Baubles, Bangles and Beads... Toys FAQ

Cage Liners: The Good, The Bad and The Ugly

Dangers of Soft PVC Toys & Vinyl Products!

Roaming

Roaming is dangerous for our slow-moving, clipped birds. Crushing injuries in birds are very difficult to repair should a bird be stepped on. A bird should be returned to the play area or cage each time he comes off the cage unless you are in the room and he is coming directly to you. If there are any side trips, he should be returned to the play area or the cage. It may take 10,000 times until he learns he is not allowed to roam. The return should be matter-of-fact. No drama, no "reward", no scolding, just a matter-of-fact return. Do not leave the room for extended periods of time when your bird is uncaged. Even the best trained bird will come off the cage and roam.

Guests

When you have guests, make sure they understand that your bird is to be given nothing to eat without your approval. Non-bird people may not understand there are foods that are toxic to birds. If you can't supervise guests, put the bird in another room. Never leave the bird unattended with the children of guests. Don't allow guests to handle the bird unless they are instructed in the proper way to handle him. It can be an important socializing tool for a pet bird to be handled by strangers, but avoid "bad" experiences.

Other Companion Animals

It is vital that other companion animals never be allowed physical contact with birds. Horror stories abound on the bird mailing lists regarding confrontations between birds and other companion animals. Some of these are:

• A dog pulled a bird from between the cage bars into pieces.

• A dog who allowed a bird to ride on his back mauled and killed the bird.

• A dog who was allowed to "kiss" a bird gave that bird a very serious bacterial infection.

• A dog pulled the tail feathers from a bird and the bird subsequently became a plucker.

• A ferret tore the throat out of a Goffin's cockatoo that fluttered to the floor while the owner was out of the room for just a minute.

• A bird who customarily chased a cat died

from septicemia when a break in the skin from the cat's claw was not discovered or considered.

Never leave your bird alone with other companion animals. Never allow the slightest physical contact with another companion animal. In any confrontation, the bird always loses....eventually. The bird may be fearless, he doesn't know his life may be in grave danger. Cage or crate other companion animals when you are away if they have the free rein of the house. They should never have access to the room where the bird is caged, whether you are home or away.

Your Bird in Another's Care

Be sure that a pet sitter or other caregiver is aware of the dangers our birds face in our homes. Along with detailed instructions for routine care and feeding, alert the sitter to the manifold opportunities for escape or injury. Inspect the bird's wing clipping and do any necessary grooming before you leave your birds in another's care. Write down some of the warning signs of potential illness for the sitter, such as loss of appetite, tail bobbing, sleeping with both feet on the perch, respiratory sounds, blood anywhere, changes in the appearance, volume or color of the feces, fluffed, excessive daytime sleeping, etc. Make arrangements with your vet for promised payment of any emergency care. Include the vet's name, phone number, and address (as well as directions to his clinic or office) in your care instructions. If the vet will give you his pager number or other emergency contact information, include this for the sitter too.

Wing Clipping

Keep the bird's wings clipped—for his safety indoors. Clipped wings do not guarantee that a bird will not escape on a gust of wind. Never take the bird out of doors unless he is in a cage or carrier. Continue to have the bird clipped or better yet, clip him yourself in the manner described in previous articles. Ankle tethers shouldn't be used on a bird.

Out of Doors

Never leave your bird unattended in a cage, enclosure or carrier out of doors. Predators, such as possums and raccoons, live in even urban settings. Snakes, cats, dogs, and biting insects are also of concern.

Windows and Mirrors

Clipping your bird and keeping him clipped will avoid injury, head trauma, and death that can occur when a bird flies full tilt into glass. Birds don't understand about glass and mirrors. They think they are a passage to the outside they see beyond. If your bird is learning to fly, draw sheers across the windows or tilt-close mini-blinds or verticals to soften the impact with glass. Paste temporary decals on mirrors. After your bird is flight proficient, clip him and keep him clipped. A bird who escapes is usually a dead bird—death by starvation, from a predator, the elements, autos, etc. Do not open doors or windows to the outside unless the bird is locked in his cage. Take the few seconds it requires to cage your bird before answering the door. Make it a practice to open any door to the outside with your back to it and the bird in plain sight.

Vet Visits and Medications

Don't permit any procedure unless you are present. Birds do not need to be anesthetized for routine grooming. Anesthesia can be risky for birds. Their respiratory systems function very differently than those of mammals. Air (and anesthesia) is circulated throughout the entire body, not just the lungs. If a vet wants to anesthetize your bird for a routine procedure, leave. Choose a vet who sees only birds, preferably a board certified one. There are many competent vets who are not board certified, but one who is may be a safer choice.

Don't give your bird antibiotics or other medications without a reason. Don't give your bird over-the-counter medications for some fancied malady. These are, for the most part, worthless. Be sure you understand the reason and the need for any medication. There is no reason to give a bird antibiotics in the absence of evidence of a disease process or an infection. Antibiotics kill bacteria, not viruses.

Have the blood calcium level checked at each annual exam. The level can change over time. African Greys, unlike many other species, are very sensitive to inadequate levels of calcium in the blood. They will have seizures or falling episodes, whereas other species may suffer fractures from inadequate calcium in their bones. Don't give calcium supplements routinely or just in case. Never give a calcium supplement in the absence of a diagnosis of abnormally low blood levels of calcium. A bird that is on a pelleted diet shouldn't require additional calcium. He needs only the calcium in the foods he gets if his blood calcium level is in the normal range.

Bird Fairs, Expos, Marts, Pet Stores, Bird Clubs

Some of the really dangerous and life threatening diseases that affect birds are brought home to them after contact, peripheral or otherwise, with birds of unknown health status. If a toy can't be run through the dishwasher, don't buy it. Leave the bags and package wrapping that you bring from a fair outside the house—do not bring them into the house. Put any toys you buy in the dishwasher after you have disrobed in the garage, put your

clothes in the washer and showered and washed your hair. Take these precautions any time you have contact with the birds of others. Needless to say: Do not take your bird to gatherings where he will be exposed to the birds of others.

PBFD apparently does not cause disease in birds over 3 year of age. Dr. Branson Ritchie was unable to experimentally infect a bird over 3 years of age when he was doing PBFD research.

Until and unless there are vaccines for the life threatening and death dealing diseases that affect our birds, we must guard them carefully from exposure. Vaccinate your bird against polyomavirus and boost yearly. Most older birds do not die from polyoma but some do. Don't let your bird be one of those.

Routine bathing is a must. But caution must be taken to assure that the water is the proper temperature. Do not leave a bird unattended near any open water.

Bathing

Baths are important for the health and well being of your bird. Our homes are, for the most part, a desert environment. Heating dries out our homes in the winter; air conditioning removes the moisture from the air in the summer. Many parrots evolved in the tropical regions of the world and require adequate skin and feather hydration.

Molting is often a time when a bird begins to pluck. They are itchy and uncomfortable with the emergence of new feathers. If they are accustomed to daily baths, this period will be easier for them and for you. Some like it, some hate it, some tolerate it, and some huddle in misery waiting for it to be over. Bathing is one of life's little miseries for some birds, but it is important and must be done. Make an effort to discover your bird's bathing preference. Some tolerate spray bathing, some like to go in the shower with you, some will bathe in the sink, some like a pan of water. If they like none of these, choose the one they hate the least.

Interaction between birds of dissimilar size and species can pose a serious hazard.

Rope & Fabric Toys

Entanglement is a very real threat to our birds. Entanglement in frayed fabric or rope can cause the loss of a toe, leg, wing.....even death. Rope and fabric items should be supervised only items. These toys or items shouldn't be left in the cage unsupervised or overnight. Deaths and infections from obstruction of the digestive system of rope and fabric fibers, especially the fabric sleeping huts, have been reported. The Cotton Candy preening toy has been implicated in reported deaths and injury on the bird mailing lists. Inspect rope toys and other fabric items frequently. Trim off any raveled fibers or threads. One of my former Cockatoo babies got frayed rope threads wrapped around his ankle. The blood supply to the foot was cut off and the bird lost his toes. At present, the only rope toy components I consider safe are short pieces of sisal. Dangling ropes, chains, thin rawhide laces, etc. also present an entanglement danger when hung from the cage bars.

Cage Crock/Bowl Holders

Do not leave crock or bowl holders empty in the cage. These rings are an invitation to exploration and entrapment. Serious injuries can occur; to the bird and to the owner who attempts to extricate the bird.

Buy spare crock or bowls and put them in the rings immediately when you remove the used crocks or bowls and fill them with foot toys or small toys.

Bird/Bird Interaction

Birds of dissimilar size, age, disposition or species should not be allowed to share a play area or interact. The life of the smaller, less aggressive, younger bird is in danger in these kinds of situations. While interaction may proceed without harm for months or years, the potential for injury is very real. Each bird needs his own cage and own play area.

Sleeping With Birds

Sleeping or napping with a bird presents a mortal danger to birds that have neither the strength nor stamina to save themselves when a sleeping human rolls over onto them. Suffocation is the result when a bird's chest is constricted.

Toys! Toys! Toys!

Playtime and toys are very important to our birds. In the wild, they can swing, fly, climb, chew, and play. These juvenile playful activities are vital for birds to mature into successful adults; the same instincts propel our companion birds. Playtime builds muscle, develops coordination, and provides an energy outlet–in the wild and in captivity.

If left to his own imagination, alone in his cage, to develop "games", a bored Grey may chew on his toes, worry the closed band, or begin to chew or pluck feathers.

Choose appropriately sized toys; small toys intended for small birds aren't sturdy enough for the larger Grey. Small parts of toys can be swallowed or become lodged on or in the beak.

Choose toys based on the activities your bird prefers. If he loves bells, choose toys with safe bells on them. The clappers can be removed and a small stainless steel quick link substituted. No toys with "jingle bells" should be offered unless the bird is very young and is very closely supervised during play. No toys with "jingle bells" should be placed inside the cage.

If your bird prefers chewing, offer a selection of brightly colored wooden toys. Destroying wood is a natural instinct for a cavity nesting bird. Chewing will also keep the beak in tip-top condition. Wood fragments of toys can cause serious obstruction problems in the crop or digestive system, and possibly death. Your bird should be observed carefully to make sure he isn't ingesting the wood.

Carefully select toys using safety as your number one criteria. Fasteners come in

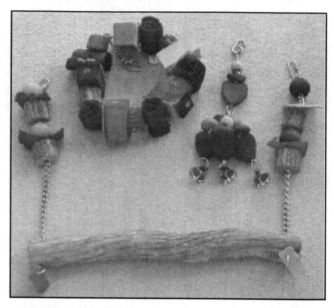

Different textures, shapes and sizes of toys stimulate your birds playtime.

many different styles. Some toy companies use the dog leash or key ring type fasteners. These are dangerous. These fasteners can be opened and the bird may get a toe, tongue, or beak caught. The safest fastener is the stainless steel quick link. If the toy you purchase doesn't have one, you can get a replacement link at most hardware, building supply, or marine supply stores. Replace any suspect fasteners with stainless steel ones. Verify with the manufacturer that metal parts on toys don't have zinc in them. Zinc poisoning has become much too prevalent in our birds.

Chains used in toys should have closed links so that a toe or tongue or beak can't get caught. Choose toys with heavy thick short chains to avoid entanglement.

Don't buy a toy that has suede (tanned chemically) or one with red leather (tanned with hemlock) on it. Wetting your finger and touching the leather can easily identify vegetable tanned leather. The moisture will leave a mark. If the leather is dyed, it should dyed be with a vegetable dye for safety. Undyed pieces of leather are usually very stiff. Toys with leather parts shouldn't be soaked in disinfectant because the leather will absorb the disinfectant and make the toy unusable. Most toys can be run through the dishwasher, on the top shelf. However, rawhide rope or lace toy parts will become quite fragile and break easily if run through the dishwasher.

The brightly colored acrylic toys are durable, dishwasher-safe, and readily ac-

cepted. Any sharp edges on acrylic toys can be filed smooth. The acrylic toy parts should be sturdy, not flimsy or bendable. Remove all suspect metal parts from these toys and replace them with stainless steel quick links, or some appropriately sized stainless steel "noise maker" from a hardware or marine supply store. If your bird begins to chip away at the acrylic, remove the toy to prevent ingestion.

Swings are well loved by most birds. The swings with two point connectors are more stable than thc ones that have a single attachment connector. The size of the branch, within reason, isn't very important. A very large branch on a swing can provide yet another perching surface and contribute to foot and toe exercise. Many of the swings have "toys" along the arms of the swings. The "toys" can be colored wood, rawhide wedges, rolls or squares, short lengths of sturdy plastic chain, heavy plastic or acrylic beads, etc.

Rope toys or preening toys are very dangerous. Deaths and serious injury have been reported with rope toys. Ingested rope can cause death from intestinal tract obstruction. Don't allow your bird access to rope toys when he is alone in his cage. Inspect toys with any rope components daily and trim away any frayed portion. Don't buy toys with rope parts that have a nylon, wire, or plastic core. Short lengths of sisal rope on toys appear to bc safe— at least there have been no reports of death, obstruction, or entanglement on the Internet bird mailing

Any toys although not dangerous in themselves, can pose a danger if not monitored carefully.

lists. Don't give your bird fabric toys of any kind.

Never hang a toy from the cage by a raw-hide lace or other thin rope. The bird could get the hanger wrapped around his neck or leg during vigorous play. Birds have lost toes, legs, wings, and their lives from en-tanglement in these types of laces or thin ropes. VERY thick pieces of SHORT rawhide rope appear to be safe.

Wood, rawhide, and leather can harbor bacteria if droppings are allowed to re-main on them. Some toy parts can be lightly sanded to re-move the soil; most can be cleaned in the dishwasher.

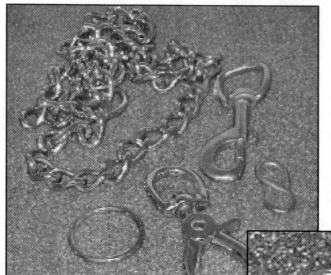

The fasteners above are dangerous for exotic birds and can cause serious injury. Chains can also be dangerous.

Quick-links (right) are safe alterna-tives to the above fasteners.

Toys should be run through the dishwasher if purchased at a bird fair, pet store, or other places where there are birds. Mail order via the Internet is very easy, and may be the safest way to purchase toys for your birds.

"Busy Work" For Greys

Roll up a small booklet such as the TV Guide and wedge it between the cage bars.

Remove the ink barrel from a ballpoint pen for a toy.

Buy a package of the flavored "pencils" for birds.

Wrap small safe toys or treats in newspaper or brown paper and place in a small card-board box on the floor of the cage.

Fill the bottom of the cage with the small unwaxed Dixie cups.

Place colored replacement parts for toys or small plain pine chunks or shapes in the bottom of the cage.

Wad up sheets of newspaper and fill the bottom of the cage.

Place small size unfinished baskets constructed of bird-safe materials in the bottom of the cage.

Place various sizes of disin-fected bird-safe branches with the bark left on in the cage.

Tie twisted pa-per towels to the cage bars.

If your bird in-gests any of these items, he can't, of course, have them. Initially offer them when you are home and can supervise his play. Greys whose owners work or who are away from home for ex-tended periods of time should provide lots of "busy work" for their birds.

Toys are meant to be used, abused, and de-stroyed. Keep a good selection on hand and rotate them often.

Diet And The Companion Grey

The nutritional requirements for birds in captivity, or in the wild, are not known. Feeding trial research, advances in avian medicine, long term captive breeding, and the keeping of companion birds is generating important new information on nutrition. One basic belief is that by feeding our birds a wide variety of foods, we can ensure that they enjoy long and healthy lives.

It is reasonable to assume that Greys, like other living creatures, require adequate amounts of protein, essential fatty acids, amino acids, vitamins, and minerals. While the interrelationships of diet constituents can be extrapolated to all psittacine species to some degree, care must be taken to accommodate species' nutritional differences. A diverse diet provides a balanced and natural means of obtaining the necessary elements. Such a diet includes pellets, fresh fruits and vegetables, "birdie bread" (see recipe), a modest amount of dry seeds for adult birds, a beans/grains mix (see recipe), and sprouts or soaked seeds.

Health, longevity, and breeding success are profoundly affected by the consumption of necessary nutrients.

Dietary Requirements

Protein

The recommended percentage of dietary protein for companion birds is 12%. Excessive protein can cause serious problems for birds whose traditional diets contain minimal levels of protein. The ancient diet was modest in protein and that is the diet our birds have evolved to handle. Grey Parrots, at least anecdotally, seem to be more sensitive to, and adversely affected by, high protein levels in the diet.

High protein foods may cause gout in birds and an increase of uric acid in the blood. This is a life threatening condition if uncorrected. Often an increase in water consumption accompanies the condition, as the body attempts to rid itself of protein by-products. The careful owner will note how much water his bird normally consumes and seek competent medical care when consumption increases. Subtle symptoms sometimes indicate a potentially serious health problem.

Beta Carotene

Birds need a continuous supply of beta carotene (a precursor to Vitamin A) for health and for a healthy immune system. Birds evolved in a habitat where beta carotene-containing foods were plentiful. Beta carotene is safe and does not have the potential for toxicity that Vitamin A supplements have. Beta carotene is found in dark green/yellow/orange fruits and vegetables and is a very important part of a bird's daily diet.

Beta carotene is not only necessary for vision, shiny feathers, and intensity of color but plays a critical role in maintaining healthy mucous membranes in the sinuses, the entire digestive tract, and the reproductive system. The lining cells of these membranes are the body's first line of defense against viruses and bacteria.

Yellow-orange and dark green vegetables are excellent sources of beta carotene, which is converted to Vitamin A in digestion. Most of the fruits and vegetables listed below may be lightly cooked or served raw. They can also be chopped or pureed and used in "birdie bread". The leafy greens, such as kale, chicory, beet, collard, mustard and turnip greens, can be chopped and added to "birdie bread" if your bird will not eat them raw.

Beta carotene rich foods: cooked acorn, butternut and Hubbard squash, cooked beet, turnip and mustard greens, carrots, kale, cantaloupe, mango, hot and sweet red peppers

Most fruits and vegetables are more nutritious raw or slightly cooked. Most vitamins are affected by heat. As a general rule, the darker the flesh, the more nutritious.

Vitamin C

Vitamin C plays an important role in maintaining a healthy immune system, improves calcium and iron absorption from the food eaten, and is necessary for the body's metabolic functioning. The safest way to ensure your bird has sufficient amounts of this important vitamin is through the bird's diet. Serving fruits and vegetables fresh will preserve their Vitamin C content. Raw spinach may interfere with calcium absorption and should be served in moderation. Include some of the foods listed below in the daily diet. According to Avian Medicine, there is no demonstrated requirement for dietary Vitamin C in birds.

Vitamin C rich foods: broccoli, brussel sprouts, cauliflower, citrus fruits, kale, kiwi fruit, mango, dark-green salad greens, spinach.

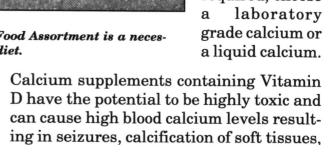

These foods are rich in Vitamin A. Food Assortment is a necessary ingredient to a well balanced diet.

Calcium

Calcium is the body's most important mineral. It is needed for healthy bones; it is essential to the blood clotting process; it helps maintain muscle control; it is involved in other life-sustaining processes.

Birds have thin, hollow bones throughout most of their bodies. Our birds don't have the calcium reserves that mammals store in their dense bones. Low blood levels of calcium can cause convulsions, irregular heartbeat, and death. Too much protein or fat interferes with the body's ability to absorb calcium. High protein and seed diets are dangerous for Greys. Avoid calcium sources such as bone meal, dolomite, oyster shells, mineral blocks, or cuttlebone. If a supplement is required, choose a laboratory grade calcium or a liquid calcium.

Calcium supplements containing Vitamin D have the potential to be highly toxic and can cause high blood calcium levels resulting in seizures, calcification of soft tissues, kidney stones, and increased lead absorption.

Megadoses or unnecessary supplementation of calcium are dangerous and life threatening. For a companion bird, use a calcium supplement only as directed by an avian vet following a diagnosis of low blood calcium.

Greys are quite sensitive to inadequate levels of calcium. Abnormally low blood calcium can, over time, cause irregular heartbeat, ataxia (may fall from perch), seizures, or death. Greys should have a blood calcium level test annually. Calcium levels can change over time and an annual measurement is necessary to ensure that the bird doesn't slip below normal. A diet high in fat interferes with calcium absorption.

Birds with calcium blood levels marginally below normal can be fed calcium-rich foods, and that may be enough to bring the level up. After several months of diet-related calcium intake, a blood calcium level test can be run to see if the diet is making a difference. If not, you may have to supplement. Any supplementation should be done under the supervision of an avian vet and only after a blood calcium level test is run.

Calcium and Vitamin D must be treated with respect. They are necessary for life; however, excessive amounts will kill. Excessive calcium supplementation can cause calcification of the internal organs and death.

Greys need enough calcium—not extra calcium. The list below demonstrates many calcium-containing foods that are readily available.

• Beans and peas: black beans, black-eyed peas, garbanzo beans, Great Northern beans, lentils, dried lima beans, Pinto beans.

• Grains: wheat, quinoa, oats, amaranth (a very glutinous grain).

• Vegetables: broccoli, summer squash, green garden peas, carrots, acorn squash, kale, figs, collard, beet and turnip greens.

• Nuts: almonds, filberts, pistachio nuts, walnuts.

• Soy milk, from which Tofu is made, is richer than cow's milk in calcium.

• Yogurt and low fat cheese.

B Vitamins

Dried beans and peas are rich sources of the important B vitamins. On a per-serving basis, beans and peas are a bargain. The protein in them, when combined with grains, is in the form of complex carbohydrates, starches, complex sugars, and dietary fiber. Soybeans (from which Tofu is made) are the best source of protein among the widely grown legumes. However, soybeans, dried lima beans, and kidney beans should be well cooked to deactivate enzymes that can cause digestive upset. Important amino acids are in relatively good supply in some beans and some peas. Providing a wide variety and combining beans and peas will ensure that all of the amino acids are available in the diet.

Fat

In the wild, the fruit of the palm oil tree, which is high in fat, is a seasonal staple of the Grey Parrot's diet. We know little about the other native foods the wild ones eat. Since companion and breeding Greys are not as active as their wild brethren, they may be unable to handle these high fat and high calorie levels in captivity. However, based on the high fat levels in the wild diet, it may be assumed that Greys need a moderate amount of dietary fat. The estimated fat requirement for birds in general is 4% to 5% daily in the diet, but species differences in dietary requirements surely exists. Dietary fat is necessary for utilization of the fat-soluble vitamins A, D, E, and K.

Dietary Recommendations

Balance in All Things

A widely varied, pellet-based diet is the best choice for a companion Grey. A diet of 100% pellets is boring. Birds enjoy taste, texture, color, and shape in their diets. A diet of 50% pellets and 50% soft foods should satisfy the gourmet in every bird. Seeds have a role in the diet–a very small role. They can be offered to adult birds in a small quantity, perhaps a tablespoon, once or twice a week. Birds under one year of age shouldn't be offered dry seeds. They need time to become accustomed to, and prefer, a varied diet.

Added vitamin and mineral supplements are not needed if the bird's diet is pellet-based. Over supplementing is dangerous. The fat-soluble vitamins are retained in the body and can cause serious health problems and death if amounts in gross excess of the body's requirements are given.

Recently weaned birds, companion birds under one year of age, sick birds, underweight birds and birds undergoing a molt should be fed fewer fresh fruits and veggies. These foods don't contain the calories that are needed for special or age-related situations.

Pellets

Pellets are recommended because they are the food most likely to fill a bird's nutritional needs. But because they are not a "complete" food (like dog and cat food), many educated owners feel that a diet of pellets and water is inadequate as well as boring. By offering the bird a variety of pellets, he will not become rigid in his preference for only one brand of pellet.

Manufactured diets for other animal species can claim to be a complete diet because there has been adequate time to conduct long term feeding trials, over many generations and thus ascertain the "complete food". However, this is not the case with exotic birds that enjoy extremely long life spans. Short-lived avian species may be able to tolerate protein, vitamin and mineral levels that are unacceptable and dangerous for the longer lived psittacines.

Most pellets contain protein levels higher than the recommended 12%. However, if bal-anced with low protein foods such as fruits and vegetables, the overall level will be lower. Once purchased, a bag of pellets should to be broken down into plastic bags and stored in the freezer. Keep one bag in the refrigerator to use from day to day.

Soft Foods

Typical daily soft foods:

- A beans/grains/pasta/nut/veggie mix.

- Birdie bread.

- Sprouts or soaked seeds.

Soft foods will sour if left in the cage for more than a couple of hours. However, fresh orange juice squeezed over the soft foods will keep them fresh and unspoiled for many hours.

Include several of the following in the daily diet: kiwi, chopped broccoli, snow peas, garden peas or pea pods, sweet corn, pomegranates, cactus pears, melons, organically grown apples, grapes in season, cooked winter squash, sweet potatoes—whatever is in season.

Fresh fruits and vegetables should be fed in small quantities in *special needs situations*, just for variety.

Remove pits and seeds, except from squash, peppers, and melons, before serving. The peels of some tropical fruits, such as mango and papaya, can cause an allergic reaction in people and may cause problems for birds. The skins of apples and oranges may be left on after being scrubbed with a brush, detergent and hot water to remove pesticide residues as well as dirt and grime. Don't feed avocado; deaths have been reported in companion birds and in birds fed avocado experimentally. The substances that are bad for humans–sugar, salt, excess fat, alcohol, caffeine–are also bad for birds.

Soaked or sprouted seeds are a much-loved part of the daily diet. Soaking alone begins the process of life and increases the nutritional content of the seed. When the most growing is occurring, the plant is at its most nutritious.

It is best to choose grains, beans, and other foods that are organically grown. Our birds are exposed to fungicides, pesticides, and herbicides on and in the foods they eat. By choosing organically grown food whenever possible, we can keep this exposure to a minimum.

Grains are an extremely important part of a bird's diet. When they are combined with dried beans and peas, they form a complete protein. Beans, peas, and grains also supply dietary fiber that is necessary for good health.

Several of the grains listed can be incorporated in the cooked bean/grains recipe: barley, brown rice, buckwheat, corn, quinoa, rye, oats, wild rice.

Don't use cracked or dried shelled corn from a feed store or grain elevator in the beans/grains mix as there may be fungus and/or field soil in these products. Popcorn kernels are a human quality food and can be easily prepared. Place a one-pound package of popcorn kernels in a very large microwave-proof mixing bowl. Fill the bowl with water; cook in the microwave for one and one-half hours in 30-minute segments of time. Replace the absorbed water at the end of the first two 30 minute segments.

Whole grain treats such as low-sugar cookies and granola, low-salt whole grain crackers, and no-salt whole-wheat pretzels may be offered daily.

Federal guidelines recommend against honey for human babies. Honey should not be fed to our birds either, as it can contain fungi and bacteria.

Animal Products

The food items listed below may be fed occasionally and in modest amounts:

- Low-salt low-fat white cheese.

- Low-fat yogurt.

- Very lean, well-cooked chicken or turkey.

- Tuna fish packed in spring water.

- Well cooked eggs.

Remove bones, skin, and fat from meat before serving. Place the meat on the top of the other foods so it will be eaten first before it has a chance to spoil.

Federal guidelines recommend that eggs be well cooked for human consumption because of the possibility of salmonella contamination.

Zupreem Primate Biscuits

The biscuits must be very fresh and placed in the freezer immediately. Never buy the biscuits unless they are in Zupreem's original packaging.

The biscuits can be a valuable tool for promoting interaction between a bird and the owner. The frozen biscuit can be placed in a small covered dish with very hot tap water. It will become soft in about 15 minutes. Cut the biscuit into bite size pieces, place on a small plate and microwave for about 8 seconds at full power if re-warming is necessary. Each biscuit morsel must be tested for hot spots before being offered by hand to the bird. The biscuits can also be fed dry if the bird will accept them.

Summary

Common sense and balance in your choice of foods will promote good health in your companion birds. The selection of lower protein pellets will provide you with ample opportunity to include other more modest sources of protein, such as the beans/grains mix and the "birdie bread", in the daily diet.

Food And Food Preparation

Preparing your bird's morning soft foods need not be a time consuming chore. Some suggestions for cutting down on the time spent in preparation include:

• Bake winter squash in season and freeze it.

• Cube one or more of the following root veggies. Cook separately, so there will be many flavors, for ten minutes in a pot of boiling water:

• Parsnips
• Turnips
• Carrots
• Sweet potatoes

• Cook or microwave a batch of boiled popcorn kernels.

• Lightly steam and chop a head of broccoli.

• Cook a small package of pasta.

• Chop some nutmeats.

• A package of unthawed frozen mixed veggies, sweet peas, or sweet corn kernels.

Mix several of the above items in with the cooked beans and cooked grains (see recipe). Package in three-day portions and freeze.

In The Morning:

Thaw the beans/grains mix.

Thaw a small portion of the baked winter squash.

Cube fresh sweet corn if desired.

Cube a small portion of an organic apple.

Add pomegranate, kiwi, blueberries, cranberries, cantaloupe, mango, cactus pear, orange, or other seasonal fruits.

If fresh sweet corn is out of season, thaw a tablespoon of frozen corn kernels per bird and add to the soft food bowl.

Soak sprouts the day before and add a heaping tablespoon to the soft food bowl. It isn't necessary for the sprouts to have tails.

Fresh orange juice can be squeezed over the soft foods and they will stay fresh for many hours. For those who work or are away from the home after the soft foods are customarily given, they can be safely left in the cage, using the orange juice, from 9am to mid-afternoon without spoiling

For larger quantities of food—up to two quarts of soft foods—squeeze the juice of a large orange over them before serving to the birds.

Cutting Boards

Don't use the same cutting board in the preparation of meats and your bird's foods as this can lead to serious and deadly consequences. The bird's food shouldn't be exposed to the bacteria from meats of any kind. Use layers of paper towels to pad the board when cutting fruits and vegetables rather than using the bare cutting board. Better still, use a specially designated board for your bird's fruits and veggies that is not used for any other purpose.

Run cutting boards through the dishwasher frequently. Add a few drops of Citricidal to the dishwasher.

Summary

Prepare your bird's foods as carefully and hygienically as you would prepare food for your family. Choose clean unblemished fruits and veggies, organically grown if possible, for your bird. Carefully inspect sprouts, nuts, grains, and seeds for insect damage and the presence of mold. Store these foods in the freezer to avoid insect infestation or the hatching of insect larvae, to prevent fat from becoming rancid, and to preserve freshness. Packaged nutmeats,

intended for baking, may be safer and cleaner than nuts in the shell. Never feed peanuts intended for animal consumption to your bird. If you feed a seed mixture, remove all peanuts before offering it to your bird.

Nutritious Foods For A Healthy Bird

For a healthy happy bird, feed a varied, nutritious, and psychologically satisfying diet. Foods vary, sometimes significantly, in their nutritional content.

28.350 grams = one ounce

Beans

Cooked per 100 grams	Calcium
Black beans	27
Black-eyed peas	23
Garbanzo beans	49
Great Northern beans	68
Green peas	26
Lentils	19
Lima beans (large)	17
Lima beans (baby)	29
Pinto beans	48

Vegetables
Cooked (except as noted)

per 100 grams	Calcium	Vitamin A
Acorn squash	44	428
Beets	16	4
Beet greens	114	510
Broccoli (cooked)	46	139
Broccoli (raw)	48	154
Butternut squash	41	700
Carrots (cooked)	31	2455
Carrots (raw)	27	2813
Cauliflower	16	2
Chicory (raw)	100	400
Collard greens	119	313
Corn, sweet, yellow	2	28
Corn, sweet, white	2	0.0
Corn, yellow, kernels	7	47
Corn, white, kernels	7	0.0
Dates	32	5
Figs (dried)	144	13
Green garden peas	27	60
Hubbard squash	17	604
Jalapeno peppers	10	22
Kale	72	740
Mustard greens	74	303
Peppers, hot chili, green	18	77
Peppers, hot chili, red	18	1075
Peppers, sweet, green	9	63
Peppers, sweet, red	9	570
Peppers, sweet, yellow	10	24
Pumpkin	15	108
Romaine (raw)	36	260
Spaghetti squash	21	11

(vegetables continued)	Calcium	Vitamin A
Spinach	146	778
Sweet potatoes	16	6636
Summer squash (yellow)	27	29
Summer squash (scallop)	15	9
Turnip greens	137	550
Zucchini	13	24

Grains

Cooked per 100 Grams	Calcium
Amaranth	154
Buckwheat	18
Barley, Pearled	11
Millet	3
Oats	54
Quinoa	60
Rice, Brown & White	10
Winter wheat	29

Fruits Raw per 100 grams	Calcium	Vitamin A
Apple	7	5
Banana	6	8
Blackberries	32	16
Blueberries	6	10
Cantaloupe	11	322
Cranberries	7	5
Kiwi	26	18
Kumquats	44	30
Mango	10	389
Orange	40	21
Papaya	24	28
Pear	11	2
Pomegranate	3	0.0
Prickly Pears	56	5
Prunes	51	199
Raspberries	22	13
Strawberries	14	3

Nuts per 1 tablespoon	Fat	Calcium
Almonds	14.802	75.411
Cashews	13.14	12.758
Filberts	17.785	53.298
Hickory nuts	18.249	17.294
Pecans	19.176	10.206
Pine nuts	14.373	7.371
Pistachio nuts	13.719	38.273
Walnuts, Black	16.04	16.443
Walnuts, English	17.54	26.649

Source: USDA Nutrient Data Laboratory
http://www.nal.usda.gov/fnic/cgi-bin/nut_search.pl

Grains: Delicious and Healthy Too

Grains are a blessing for bird owners. They are that rare combination, a nutritious food that birds also love. There are many varieties of grains, each providing somewhat different nutritional value. As a group, they are low in fat and packed with proteins, complex carbohydrates, vitamins, and minerals. Prepared properly, birds love the taste of the individual kinds of grains.

Grains can be offered, along with pellets, veggies, and fruit to increase the variety in a bird's diet.

Buy organically grown grains from the health food store. Add pasta, veggies, nuts, cooked dried beans, or other ingredients to the mix. When grains are combined with beans, the combination forms a complete protein. Spray the cooking pot with PAM before measuring out the water into it so the grains won't stick to the pot. Store all grains in the freezer.

Beans Mix · Center: Triticale · Pearl Barley · Millet · Brown Rice

hibits cholesterol production in the blood of humans has been traced to the non-fibrous portion of the grain.

To cook Pearled Barley: add 1 measure of pearled barley to 2 measures of boiling water, lower heat, cover and simmer for about 20 minutes.

Buckwheat Groats – Buckwheat is an excellent source of complex carbohydrates. It also contains a high proportion of all eight amino acids that the body doesn't manufacture but which are essential for good health. Buckwheat is closer to being a complete protein than any other plant source—even soybeans.

To cook Buckwheat Groats: add 1 measure of buckwheat groats to 2 measures of water. Bring to a boil, lower heat, cover, and simmer for about 20 minutes.

Bulgar – Bulgar contains goodly amounts of protein and carbohydrates as well as generous amounts of calcium, thiamin, riboflavin, and niacin.

To cook Bulgar: add 1 measure of bulgar to 2 measures of water. Bring to a boil, lower heat, cover, and simmer for 20-25 minutes.

Grains

Pearled Barley – A cup of cooked barley offers the same amount of protein as a glass of milk, along with hearty increments of niacin and thiamin. A substance that in-

Hulled Millet – Millet is low in fat and rich in riboflavin. It is higher in the amino acid lysine than rice, corn, or oats.

To cook Millet: add 1 measure of millet to 2 measures of water. Bring to a boil, lower heat, cover, and simmer for 20 minutes. Allow to stand off heat, covered for 10 minutes.

Wheat Berries – Wheat is high in protein, carbohydrates, B vitamins, and seven of the amino acids that provide the body with energy.

To cook Wheat Berries: add 1 measure of wheat berries to 2 measures of boiling water. Simmer for about an hour or until the wheat is soft, adding water as necessary.

Quinoa – Quinoa is jam-packed with lysine and healthy amounts of the other amino acids that make a protein complete. It contains calcium, vitamin E, and assorted B vitamins.

To cook Quinoa: add 1 measure of quinoa to 2 measures of water. Bring to boil, lower heat, cover, and simmer for 15 minutes. Allow to stand off heat, covered, for 10 minutes.

Triticale – a hybrid grain of wheat and rye, Triticale contains a better balance of amino acids than either wheat or rye.

To cook Triticale: add 2 measures of water to 1 measure of triticale. Bring to a boil, lower heat, cover, and simmer until the triticale is soft; adding water as needed.

There are as many ways to serve the grains to your birds as there are people to devise them. The following recipe combines grains with pasta, beans, nuts, and vegetables. The grains and veggies can be varied from batch to batch. Experiment to find the combination that your birds prefer.

Grains, Pasta, & Veggie Mix

• 1 cup each of several different grains. Cook separately so there will be many flavors.

• 1 cup cooked pasta (Orzo or other small pasta); roughly chop several hot peppers into the cooking water.

• 1 cup brown rice (If using white rice, season with 1 tablespoon of cinnamon.)

• A wide variety of cooked dried beans and peas. Roughly chop a head of garlic or a handful of green or red hot peppers into the cooking water.

Add several of the following:

• broccoli - steamed lightly and chopped

• small bag of frozen sweet peas - don't thaw

• small bag frozen sweet corn - don't thaw

• toasted unsalted sunflower kernels

• chopped nuts

• dried cranberries, blueberries, cherries

• mango, papaya, or other dried fruits, chopped

This recipe will make a very large batch. Owners with a few birds may prefer to use half, or less, of the suggested portions of the ingredients.

Package in freezer baggies in 3 day portions—about the maximum time it is safe in the refrigerator. Baggies of the mix can be stored frozen for an indefinite period.

Offer about 2 tablespoons per meal to bigger birds, and about 1 tablespoon for the smaller birds.

Sprouts: Nutritious And Easy To Grow

Sprouting seeds, beans, peas, and grains are a natural and healthy way to provide nutrition to your birds. In addition to being an excellent source of amino acids found in living plants, they provide variety in the diet (texture, color, and taste) and can become favorites of many birds.

Sprouting is easy to do, once you've learned the procedure. And there are a large variety of grains, seeds, beans, and peas that can be used.

You can buy beans, peas, and grains for sprouting from a health food store whose bulk bins have lids, or buy the sealed packages of seeds intended for sprouting. The various sprout mix components from the bulk bins sprout as well, at a significant reduction in price.

Some seeds, beans and peas for sprouting include:

• Radish seeds
• Mung beans
• Chinese Red Peas (may be called Adzuki)
• Sunflower seeds
• Lentils
• Cabbage seeds
• Green peas (whole, not split peas)
• Garbanzo beans
• Wheat berries
• Popcorn kernels

Popcorn kernels are an excellent addition to the sprouting mix. They are a clean human quality product and sprout well, although not quickly.

Don't use any seeds intended for planting in your sprouting mix. These seeds are pretreated with fungicides or other substances so they won't rot or be eaten by insects before they germinate and grow into a garden plant.

Don't sprout soybeans, lima beans or kidney beans. They have an enzyme that needs to be inactivated by heat to avoid digestive upset.

"THE JAR" Seed Sprouter by Sprout Ease comes with three different plastic mesh tops; is affordable and easy to use. The different size holes in each top allow you to rinse everything from small seeds to sunflower seeds.

Run the sprouting jar and the plastic screen you intend to use through the dishwasher each time you begin a new batch.

Dry Sprout Storage

Combine the various grains, seeds, beans, and peas and place them in an airtight jar or in the freezer. Freezing will prevent the oil in the fatty seeds, such as the sunflower seeds and the grains, from becoming rancid during storage. Since most of the ingredients are organically grown, freezing will prevent any larvae from hatching as they might during room temperature storage. Freezing won't affect the sprouting ability of any of the various components of the mix.

Pre-soak rinsing

Place the dry sprout mix in the sprouting jar. Shake and rinse the mix vigorously in hot water several times to knock off and rinse away any grime or other debris. Often the reason that sprouts spoil is that they aren't rinsed vigorously enough before set to soak.

Overnight Soaking

Soak the mixture of seeds, beans, grains, and peas for 6 to 8 hours. Rinse with tepid water several times in the morning before serving. You don't have to wait until the sprout tails start peeking out. By soaking, you have already begun the life cycle of the seed.

Daytime Soaking

Soak the mixture of seeds, beans, grains, and peas for 6 to 8 hours. Rinse them several times during the 6-8 hours and refill the jar with hot water each time. At the end of the soaking period, rinse well and prop the jar at a 45-degree angle so the water will drain away. Gently shake the jar after each rinse to spread out the mix onto the side of the jar. Rinse several times with warm water during the day to keep the mix moist. Reprop the jar after each rinse and allow to sit overnight. Rinse several times in the morning before serving.

If the sprout mix has tails, be very gentle when rinsing so that you don't damage the sprout tails. Serve them short tails rather than long tails. A quarter inch or less is a nice length for the sprout tails. If they develop roots or leaves, don't feed them—they will be bitter.

Soaking or sprouting one-third cup of the dry sprout mix should be enough for several meals if you have one medium to large bird. A heaping spoonful of sprouts can be mixed in with a slightly reduced portion of the regular soft food breakfast. Prepare more frequent batches of sprouts rather than making up one very large batch.

Sprouts are a wonderful source of low-fat nutrition for birds such as Amazons that may need to diet. And because they are so fresh, easy to prepare, and packed with nutrition, they are an excellent food for all birds.

Switching Your Bird To Pellets

This is the method that I use to switch birds from seeds to pellets:

Give the bird the usual ration of seeds and soft foods in the morning; remove the soft foods and seeds in the early afternoon. The primary pellet and small quantities of several of the samples mixed together should be available in the cage at all times. If the bird hasn't eaten any of the pellets by evening, give him another bowl of soft foods.

If the bird isn't eating soft foods, two portions of seeds will have to be offered daily until he is eating the pellets and/or the soft foods. Some birds will starve themselves rather than eat pellets or soft foods instead of seeds so closely observe the bird's food consumption.

If he is eating soft foods, the transition will be much easier because he can be offered soft foods twice daily and you can be assured he is getting sufficient healthy nourishment while waiting for him to accept the pellets.

Healthy soft foods such as a "birdie bread", a beans/grains mix, sprouts, cooked sweet potatoes, cooked winter squash, boiled popcorn kernels, fresh fruits and veggies high in Vitamin A should be offered during this transition—and as a permanent part of the diet. I don't recommend a 100% pellet diet.

Germinated seeds or sprouts are a good transition food as they resemble the dry seeds enough that the bird will usually eat them readily. Requesting samples from the pellet manufacturers can provide a varied

supply of pellets for the bowl. The bird may prefer one pellet over another. Even if he chooses only one, continue to add a small amount of the other samples to the pellet bowl. It is important for the bird to see a variety of shapes, colors, and sizes in his bowl.

It can sometimes take months or even years to make the switch. Be patient and continue to offer the pellets. Eventually the bird will nibble on them—from curiosity or hunger while waiting for his next portion of seeds or soft foods.

A cold turkey switch is not recommended. This is much too stressful and can cause behavior problems in companion birds brought on by hunger, anxiety, frustration, and deprivation.

The brand of pellet the bird chooses at this point isn't especially important. There are questions in the minds of some bird keepers whether artificial preservatives and dyes are healthy for birds. Seeds are such a nutritionally deficient diet that almost any pellet is better. With patience and persistence, the bird can be gradually switched over to a "healthier" pellet—one containing no preservative or dyes. While most preservatives and dyes in most pellets are human quality, even some humans are sensitive to them. One supposes this may be true for birds too.

Weigh your companion bird daily during the switch from seeds to pellets. Watch the feces carefully. It should not be scanty or black. Check the waste tray to see if there are pellet crumbs or the eaten remains of any of the soft foods. Check the water bowl to see if there are pellet crumbs.

Choose a base pellet for the initial conversion which doesn't contain chemical preservatives or artificial coloring, such as Harrison's Bird Diet, Ziegler's, or Hagen's

Tropican. Small quantities of other pellets, perhaps a teaspoon, can be added.

Call the pellet manufacturers and ask for samples. Use these samples as a small portion of the pellets that are offered. The 800 numbers for some of the food manufacturers are listed below.

800-353-2473 Diamond Avian

800-225-2700 Hagen

800-346-0269 Harrison's Bird Diet

800-543-3308 L'Avian

800-842-6445 Lafeber (some products)

800-332-5623 L/M Animal Farm

800-356-5020 Pretty Bird International

800-326-1726 Roudybush Feed

800-327-7974 Scenic

800-345-4767 Zupreem

Soft foods:

Please refer to the articles <u>Grains: Delicious and Healthy Too, Sprouts: Nutritious and Easy To Grow</u>, to the Birdie Bread and Beans/Grain recipes.

Other soft food recipes can be found at the BirdsnWays Recipe Xchange[1].

URLs found in Recommended Reading

Treats Your Birds Will Enjoy

Bobbi's Birdie Bread

2 boxes of Jiffy Corn Muffin Mix

3 tablespoons of baking powder

1 teaspoon of Earthrise Spirulina

2 eggs and shells (puree in blender)

4 jars of baby foods (4 ounce or 113 gram jars)

Three-quarter cup of peanut butter

2 cups of dry baby cereal

1 and one-half cups of shredded/chopped veggies (usually carrots or broccoli)

Mix wet and dry ingredients separately.

Combine wet and dry ingredients along with the shredded/chopped veggies.

Spray a 9x13 inch pan with Pam Cooking Spray. Bake for about 30 minutes (check for doneness) in a 400 degree F. pre-heated oven.

Cool slightly on a rack, cut into squares and freeze in a freezer zip-lock plastic bags.

Choose baby food fruits and veggies a high vitamin A content.

Two jars of veggies, such as sweet potatoes, squash, carrots, mixed vegetables.

One jar of a fruit.

One jar of a meat, such as chicken or turkey with rice, veggies, or noodles.

Jiffy Corn Muffin Mix substitute:

2 boxes = 12.5 ounces of yellow cornmeal and 4.5 ounces of flour.

or

2 boxes = 360 grams of yellow cornmeal and 120 grams of flour.

Conversions:

1 tablespoon = 9 grams

1 teaspoon = 3 grams

1 cup = 240 grams

400 degrees F. = 204 degrees C.

1 inch = 2.54 centimeters

1 ounce = 28.350 grams

Beans, Grains, Pasta, Veggie Mix

Boiled Popcorn Kernels

Bobbi's Birdie Bread

Boiled Popcorn Kernels

Microwave

Place one pound of popcorn kernels in a very large microwave proof bowl.

Microwave on high for one and one-half hours in 30-minute increments, adding water as needed to cover the popcorn kernels.

Drain, cool and add to beans mix or package in 3-day servings and freeze.

Crockpot

Place one pound of popcorn kernels in crockpot.

Fill pot with water, cover, set on low, and cook overnight.

Drain, cool, and add to beans mix or package in 3-day servings and freeze.

Stovetop

Place one pound of popcorn kernels in a large heavy pot.

Cover kernels with water, bring to a boil, lower heat, and simmer until kernels are soft. Add water as needed to cover popcorn kernels.

Drain, cool, and add to beans mix or package in 3-day servings and freeze.

Beans, Grains, Pasta, Veggie Mix

Approximately 20 ounces or 567 grams package of mixed beans & peas

several different kinds of grains

1 cup of small pasta

small package of frozen sweet corn kernels or mixed veggies.

Wash beans and peas and place in a large heavy pot.

Add water to a depth of several inches over the surface of the beans and peas.

Bring to a boil, remove from heat, cover, and let sit for 1 hour.

Bring back to a boil, uncovered, and simmer for 40 minutes.

Stir frequently.

Drain beans and cool

Add several roughly chopped hot peppers or dried hot pepper pods to the cooking water of the beans and to the pasta water.

Cook all grains in separate pots (see the article Grains: Delicious and Healthy Too).

Combine ingredients. Freeze in plastic freezer bags in 3-day portions.

Optional additions to the mix:

Chopped nuts

Frozen sweet green peas

Chopped dried fruit

Toasted unsalted sunflower kernels

Boiled popcorn kernels

Your birds will enjoy sharing your popped corn. No butter or salt, please.

Quick & Easy Beans, Grains, Pasta, Veggie Mix

Combine:

1) Two pounds of brown rice.

2) Four different varieties of Near East grain products (including the flavor packet). Some of the Near East mixes include Roasted Garlic, Roasted Pecan & Garlic, Almond Pilaf, and Coucous Toasted Pine Nut. www.NearEast.com

3) One-quarter cup each of several grains such as pearled barley, buckwheat groats, oat groats, quinoa, triticale, bulgar, hulled millet, etc. If too many of these grains are added, the mixture will cook up wet instead of fluffy.

4) Combine, mix well, and store in a freezer bag in the 'fridge.

Cook the rice, Near East varieties, and grains mixture using one and three-quarter cup of water for each cup of the combined grains mixture.

Cook these ingredients separately:

1) One pound of popcorn kernels (see the boiled popcorn kernel recipe).

2) 20 ounces of a wide variety of dried beans and peas. Add a handful of chopped hot peppers or a head of chopped garlic to the bean cooking water for flavoring. Add frozen greens such as turnip, collard, or mustard and at least one package of frozen broccoli during the last 10 minutes of cooking. Simmer until beans are cooked through but not soft and mushy.

3) One pound of pasta. Add a handful of chopped hot peppers or a head of chopped garlic to the pasta cooking water for flavoring.

After draining the beans, the pasta, and the cooked popcorn combine them and add a large bag of frozen mixed veggies to cool the mixture.

Add several of the following to the cooked combined beans, rice, pasta, popcorn, veggie mixture:

Toasted unsalted sunflower kernels.

Pine nuts.

Roasted unsalted pumpkin seed kernels or pepitos (squash seed kernels).

Roasted unsalted corn nuts.

Chopped nuts.

Pack into freezer bags in three day portions and freeze.

From One Breeder to Another - The African Grey

Breeding African Greys can be a very rewarding and learning experience, but it also requires an uncommon dedication. The breeding pairs, the babies, and your clients deserve an informed, committed, ethical, responsible, and knowledgeable breeder.

Breeding Greys is not just a matter of buying two birds, putting them together and letting nature take its course. Healthy and productive breeding pairs are required. Parents need the proper environment and diet to breed successfully. Chicks must be properly hand fed, weaned, and socialized in order to develop into good companion birds. More effort is required to assure that the babies go only to good homes, in educating the new owners and in keeping in touch to make sure that all is going well. All of this takes time, knowledge and extraordinary commitment and should not be entered into lightly.

Start-up expenses will be considerable. Social engagements will be planned around your feeding schedule; vacations will be very rare; holidays, birthdays, and anniversaries are just another day in the life of a breeder.

Feeding and watering the breeding pairs, cleaning cages, tidying up the aviary, routine maintenance, and handfeeding the babies comes before convenience or pleasure.

More is known today than ever before to help us meet the challenge of raising healthy, well-socialized companion birds. Given their intelligence and sensitivity, perhaps breeding and raising African Greys is the most challenging of all. Those who are drawn to this endeavor by their compassion and deep desire to nurture and contribute to the well being of these most beloved of earth's creatures will be rewarded beyond measure.

One of the most important first steps to successful breeding is a healthy pair of adult birds. Learn and understand the physical signs of healthy birds. Birds that have malformed feathers or pluck their feathers may be seriously ill. Some disease processes can cause plucking. Although plucking itself is unlikely to be inherited, the inability to handle stress as evidenced by plucking may well have a genetic component. Calm birds in good feather are obviously more desirable than terrified feather pluckers.

Other signs of ill health are a fluffed bird, a bird sitting low on the perch, respiratory sounds, tail bobbing, swelling or discharge from the eyes or nares, a pasted vent, feces containing undigested food, and abnormal color of urine, urates or feces. Although some foods can cause discoloration of the urine or the feces, the cause of any and all abnormalities should be investigated. Ideally, one should buy birds from a trusted source that agrees to make the sale conditional on a clean bill of health. Plan to pick up the birds on the way to the appointment with your avian vet. Consider taking a separate carrier for each bird.

Get as much history on the birds as possible. Previous diet, approximate age, and health history will be most useful for management purposes. If the pair is proven, the breeding history regarding the number of times per year the pair produces and the number of eggs per clutch can assist you in determining if the pair is comfortable with the way you have them set up. Find out what style of nestbox and cage size they were accustomed to before purchase.

Baseline Medical Data

A number of medical tests and procedures should be performed to ensure the birds are suitable for breeding. First, is a thorough physical examination. Surgical sexing including an examination of the internal organs can be done as necessary. Second, are bacteriologic tests such as a Gram's stain and a Culture and Sensitivity, which may be recommended based on the Gram's stain results. Some avian vets routinely do a Culture and Sensitivity instead of the Gram's Stain. Third, is a fecal flotation for the presence of worms. Worming can produce surprising results and should be considered. Last, are blood tests that should include a

Complete Blood Count, a Complete Blood Chemistry Panel, and a PBFD screen. In the event of anomalous test results or profession observations of concern, a DNA blood probe for latent or active psittacosis infection, or testing for heavy metal poisoning, or an electrophoresis screen for aspergillosis can be run. If the birds have not been vaccinated against polyomavirus, the first of the two shots can be administered at this time. If the seller will provide you with reports of past examinations, go over the reports with your avian vet or contact the seller's avian vet to discuss the records.

Essential Quarantine and Diet Strategies

The absolute minimum quarantine period is 30 to 60 days. Unfortunately, in most homes the airflow is shared and strict quarantine is impossible. Many breeders don't have an off-site or outdoors quarantine location. If the birds are a pair, quarantine them together in a large cage in an out-of-the-way area unless you can quarantine them out-of-doors. If one bird of the pair must be medicated as a result of the health examination findings, cage the birds separately until the sick bird is medicated as directed and rechecked to make sure the health problem has been corrected. If they are singles, introduce them after quarantine as you would any other potential pair.

Feed quarantine birds last, change their cages last, and keep a smock and shoes near the door for use only in the quarantine room. If the birds were on a seed diet prior to purchase, begin the change from seeds to pellets and offer a varied diet of soft foods while they are being quarantined. Pellets and soft foods are a much more nutritious diet than seeds for the pair to feed the babies. Only two of my pairs failed to begin eating the pellets during quarantine; it took me three years to get them off seed and onto pellets and soft foods. If a new pair is on a seed diet, offer soft foods and the birds' normal ration of seeds in the morning. Several kinds of pellets should be available at all times. Remove the soft foods and the seed dish in the afternoon. The birds will have pellets and water until the next morning. Eventually, from boredom or hunger, they will begin to eat the pellets. It is very important to continue giving them seeds until they accept a varied nutritious diet even if it takes several weeks, months, or years. They are in a stressful situation initially and seeds are familiar food. Familiarity of any sort reduces stress.

Cage and Nestbox Etiquette

The smallest cage I use is a 4x4x4 suspended cage constructed from 1x1 inch wire. The boot nestbox is best. Most Greys will scramble into the box when you enter the aviary unannounced. To cut down on panic, knock twice on the door, waiting between each knock, and then pause again after you open the door. The birds quickly learn they have enough time to get safely into the nestbox after this signal.

The hens will lay in the farthest corner of the "toe" of the boot, so there is little concern about the males diving into an egg-laden nest or onto the babies. The basic shape is a vertical grandfather 12x12x24 with a boot toe extension measuring 12x12x12. One by twelve inch pine planking holds up better than plywood. Another advantage of pine planking is that it doesn't contain glue or other adhesives, as does plywood, which the birds chew. Placing hunks of left over 1x12 pine plank or lengths of 2x4 on the bottom of the cage can satisfy a pair's need to chew and spare the nestbox or perches. A large chunk of a natural wood branch, thoroughly disinfected, may serve as well.

An interior wire ladder is required from the cage side bottom of the nestbox entry hole to the floor of the nestbox. It should be securely fastened at the top and bottom to avoid separation from the nestbox and so the birds don't get trapped inside or prevented from entering the box. Four inches of pine shavings can be used as nestbox substrate and should be replaced after each clutch is removed from the nestbox. A dilute solution of a bird-safe disinfectant, such as OxyFresh, Citricidal, or Kennelsol, can be sprayed on and wiped from the surface of the now empty box.

Do Not Disturb

Disturb the birds as little as possible. Pairs should feel that the nestbox is theirs alone—a safe place to raise a family. Pairs who are protective or who feel vulnerable will feel more secure if the nestbox isn't inspected at all. Closed circuit cameras can be installed to keep an eye on breeding activity. Some of the new video cameras are very small and inconspicuous. The large bulky color video cameras can be purchased second hand for under $100. Black and white surveillance cameras are intended, in many cases, for low light locations and can be very useful for observing the birds' activities. You will need a power supply (around $25) and enough co-ax cable to reach from the camera to one of your television input connections.

If the female spends the night in the nestbox, she may have layed an egg. Watch the next morning when the lights come on. If she spends two nights in the nestbox, she surely has layed. If the pair will tolerate nestbox inspection, you can check the nestbox once a week until you find the first egg; otherwise, rely on watching via the camera. Pair incompatibility, as well as human interference, can play a role in eliciting protective behavior. This protective behavior can take the form of expressions of fear, anxiety, and insecurity by excessive or prolonged growling upon inspection, hiding in the nestbox when out of the presence of the caregiver, injuries to the babies, less production, and fewer eggs. The cameras can be very useful with these pairs. Having the box checked daily before I got them disturbed one of my pairs. This particular pair, once double clutchers with two babies per clutch, has given me triple clutches with three and four babies per clutch. Their increased production can be attributed to being disturbed less; consequently they feel more secure.

Supplemental Foods

The addition of one-quarter teaspoon of Neo-Calglucon to the soft foods after the first egg is discovered will replace the calcium drawn from the hen's body for the formation of the cuticle of the egg. Supplementation should be continued until two weeks after the last egg is layed. A laying hen's blood calcium can rise to over 25 during egg laying from the normal reference values of 7.0 to 9.5 for African Greys. This indicates the massive amount of calcium that is withdrawn from the organs and the bones. Keeping accurate records for each pair can give you an idea of how many eggs you can expect to better plan when to discontinue the calcium supplementation. Since Neo-Calglucon is so safe, it is of little consequence if the pair gets it for several extra days. When the pair is feeding babies, extra calcium added to the soft foods could be hazardous to the babies. If your hen has chronically low blood calcium levels, consult your avian vet.

Spirulina is added to my "birdie bread" and Wheatgrass is sprinkled on the soft foods. The majority of soft foods, grains, sprouts, and beans are organically grown and are from the health food store. Sweet corn is well loved and eagerly consumed. My Grey breeding birds are fed Harrison's Bird Diet. No supplemental vitamins/minerals should be offered if birds are on a pellet-based diet. Birds who are on pellets and a varied soft food diet are getting all the vitamins and minerals they need unless a bird has low blood calcium. A small quantity of seeds can be offered twice a week as a treat. Breeder formulation pellets should be offered when the pair is feeding babies.

Mating to Hatching

My Greys usually copulate in the morning for about ten days before the hen lays. Once they start copulating in the evening as well, laying is imminent.

Steady and sturdy perches are important as mating often occurs over an extended period of time, on the average more than 10 minutes. Perches should be the right diameter; if they are too large or too small, the hen may be unable to sustain her balance during mating. Perches ranging in diameter from one and a half inches to three inches along the length will provide the hen with a choice for secure footing.

Some hens will benefit from a second perch positioned four inches away from the first. She will be able to lean forward and brace herself for balance and footing during mating. Breeding Greys are most comfortable if their perches are above their caretaker's head. When limited by the height of the room, lower perches will not adversely affect birds that are otherwise secure in their cage and secure in their nestbox.

If you know your birds or watch them on camera, you will have a pretty good idea of when incubation has begun and be able to calculate hatch dates within two or three days. Some hens begin incubating with the first egg; others may wait until the second egg. If the first two babies are the same age, based on development, the hen begins incubating with the second egg. If the babies are three days apart in age, based on development, the hen begins incubation with the first egg. If incubation begins with the second egg rather than the first, this can be a significant advantage if the clutch is large. The age difference between the first and last baby is not as great and there is less chance of the youngest getting lost in the shuffle. Most Greys are good parents; how they manage to feed their lazy babies, I can't even guess as it is not unusual for the handfeeder to have to wake the babies up between spoonfuls of formula.

It is important for the health and safety of the babies that the pair be provided with cage and nestbox security. In addition to video cameras, one of the best purchases you can make for monitoring activities once the babies hatch is a remote infant monitor from Radio Shack. The unit is amazingly sensitive. You can hear the parents leaving and entering the box as well as the babies making their distinctive feeding sounds. The receiving portion of the monitor can be placed against the top of the boot or hung facing the wall of the boot.

Feeding the Parents and the Babies

If the breeding pair aren't paper chewers, the bottom of the cage can be lined with newspaper when they are feeding babies. The paper can be changed three times a day to avoid the birds retrieving a spoiled morsel of food. Giving the parents an over abundance of soft foods will help them feel secure that there is plenty of food for even the largest brood. The parents and the babies in the nestbox will consume an amazing amount of food. Parent birds, provided with an abundance of nutritious foods at 8 or 9am, at 3pm, and at 9pm, will produce healthy fat babies. An hour before the lights go out, another bowl of food that won't spoil by morning should be offered such as sweet corn, sprouts, fresh fruits, and vegetables. Sprinkle of all the soft foods with Wheatgrass and provide unlimited Harrison's pellets and the babies will sprout the most beautiful fire engine red tails above the characteristic dark margins of immatures. Pellets should be available at all times. The birds will gorge themselves shortly before lights out and feed the babies during the night. In the early morning, they will finish off the bowl of food given the night before.

Don't be concerned if the hen is seen outside the nestbox infrequently. She will come out only to relieve herself, have a drink of water, or to be fed by the male when the babies are very young. When the babies are a little older, the hen may eat for herself rather than depend on the male for all of the food for her and the growing brood. The male will typically feed the hen in the box or at the entrance. If she comes out of the box for any reason, the male will often feed her then also. It is so strange to see an adult female, or any adult, with a bulging crop.

I reward the parents with dry seeds and pomegranates after pulling the babies. My pairs aren't offered seeds or pomegranates while they are feeding babies. Since the breeding birds love dry seeds and pomegranates, they would fill the babies up with them instead of the nourishing soft foods and pellets.

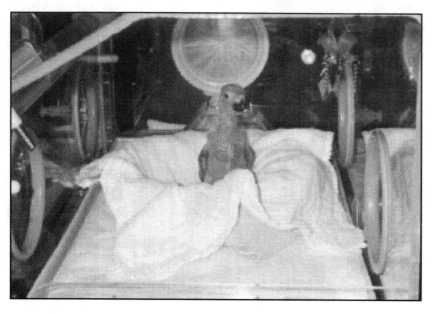

The Brooder

Cleanliness is not only next to godliness, it can mean the difference between life and death for your baby birds. The brooder should be thoroughly disinfected. A dilute bleach solution may be a good first step. Disinfectants such as OxyFresh, Citricidal and Kennelsol are effective against multiple kinds of pathogens. Flood the corners of the brooder with the disinfectant solution as well as the areas where the walls and floor meet. The brooder should be rinsed and dried after allowing the wet surface contact time the manufacturer recommends.

Before taking the babies from the nest, have your brooder all set up with the temperature and humidity regulated for at least two days prior to pulling the babies. Set the temperature initially at 90 degrees F. If there are three or four babies, that may be a little warm. If there are one or two babies, 92 degrees may be more suitable. Watch the babies—if they are panting, turn the temperature down degree by degree over several hours. Don't turn it down too much too fast or you may well miss the babies' comfort zone. Don't depend on one thermometer—use at least two. If the temperature is too low, there can be serious complications with crop emptying. When the babies are old enough to explore, the thermometers should be removed for safety's sake. The babies will be most comfortable at 55% humidity. Grey babies are well hydrated if the feces are moist and the liquid portion of the waste is about the size of a quarter.

Avian Medicine: Principles & Application by Ritchie, Harrison & Harrison recommends the following temperatures (all degrees F.):

• Day 1 to Day 7 babies: 95-97 degrees for the first week

• Unfeathered chicks: 90-92 degrees

• Chicks with some pin feathers: 85-90 degrees

• Fully feathered chicks: 75-80 degrees

• Weaned chicks: 68-75 degrees

Avian Medicine further notes: "The actual temperature should be adjusted according to the needs of the individual chick." Feather eruption is discussed in very general terms: "Feather growth occurs rapidly in neonatal birds and follows a set pattern that varies among species. In general, feather growth starts with the head, wings and tail, followed by feather emergence on the rest of the body."

All the bedding should be washed first in very hot water and detergent; after the last rinse, disinfect the bedding using the bleach/water ratio recommended on the bleach container. Set the washer timer for 15 minutes. After the last rinse, run the load through the rinse cycle again. It is important that there be no bleach residue left in the bedding. The babies' skin is very thin and fragile and does not react well to bleach residue.

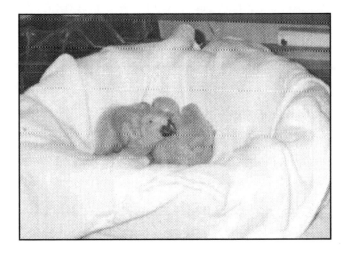

Make a "nest" for the babies in the brooder by rolling up a bath towel and forming it into a circle. Put a bath towel on the floor of the brooder for softness and place a thick pad of paper towels under the "nest". Drape a baby diaper or an infant receiving blanket over the "nest". The babies use the walls of the "nest" to rest against and the circle keeps them from straying. Place a padded container in the brooder if you have enough room so you can transfer the babies to this container when you replace the soiled bedding. To avoid chilling young babies, expose them to room temperature only when they are being fed.

If the brooder has a water well, the use of distilled water will avoid mineral buildup. Add a small quantity of Citricidal, a bird-safe disinfectant, to prevent the growth of unwanted organisms in the water well. Those who use aquariums as brooders can add humidity a couple of ways. A wet sponge in a small container is the safest. When the babies are very small and can't climb out of the circle, you can use a small quantity of Nolvasan or a couple of drops of Citricidal in a shallow container of water. The more water surface that is exposed to the air, the higher the humidity. Tap water might have cooties in it, so it is best to use a bird safe disinfectant in the humidity water and to use distilled water. The water in the container should be changed every other day or so.

Handfeeding the Babies: Concerns and Techniques

Everything that touches the babies should be disinfected including your hands. I use a laboratory hand cleaner that kills gram negative and gram positive bacteria, fungi, and yeast. Since I use a spoon and a large glass mug for feeding, these items and the metal measuring spoon can be soaked in a very strong disinfectant between feedings. Don't allow anything that goes into the babies' mouths to touch your countertop. Kitchen countertops, dish cloths, sponges, etc. can be seriously contaminated with gram negative and other pathogenic bacteria. Place a paper towel on the countertop and put the spoon or syringe on the towel.

Prepare the formula fresh with each feeding—no exceptions. If you are interrupted for longer than 15 minutes, prepare fresh formula. To prepare the formula, measure the water and dry formula powder in a large glass mug. Place the mug in a shallow baking dish and run very hot water into the dish. Some disinfectant solutions may be absorbed by plastic syringes, plastic bowls, or plastic mugs used for formula preparation or handfeeding. Non-porous handfeeding equipment avoids this possibility. OxyFresh and Citricidal are good disinfectants to use for plastics but the soaking solution will have to be changed every other day or so. Feed each clutch separately with freshly prepared formula. Several days' supply of formula can be kept in a container in the 'fridge. The balance of the formula should be frozen and the date noted when the formula went into the freezer.

Nutritionally incomplete homemade formulas can cause serious health problems and even death as described in <u>Avian Medicine: Principles & Application</u>. I have had good weight gains and healthy babies using the Kray formula made with Zupreem primate biscuits. The recipe is:

1 pound of primate biscuits (ground into powder by blender or food processor).

1 pound of ABBA Green 92 Nestling Food.

2 ounces of dry baby cereal - the mixed grain variety.

1 teaspoon of Spirulina mixed into the dry ingredients.

The following jars of baby food are the 4-ounce jars:

1 jar of green beans

2 jars of peas

1 jar of a fruit

1 jar of creamed corn

1 jar of a meat

1 jar of either carrots or squash

Mix baby foods in the blender with 2 cups of water.

Measure out 2 rounded cups of the dry mixture.

Stir dry and wet mixture; let sit for a few minutes.

Spoon the mixture into ice cube trays that have been just run through the dishwasher.

Remove and place the cubes in a freezer bag after frozen solid.

Thaw the number of cubes required for a feeding in the microwave; add a small amount of water to slightly thin; and stir down to cool.

Check the temperature of the formula with a thermometer before feeding.

For syringe feeding, the ABBA Green should be run through the food processor for a smoother formula mix.

Use only Zupreem brand in the original packaging for the primate biscuit portion of the recipe. The biscuits, and the dry blend of ingredients in the formula base, should be frozen until used in the recipe.

Avian medical literature covers crop burn, crop stasis, splay leg, stunting, aspiration, constricted toe syndrome, pendulous crop, and other problems. A breeder MUST know how to recognize and avoid these conditions. Be diligent in learning about these conditions for the sake of the babies. This level of medical knowledge is the basic information without which a breeder should reconsider his acceptability as a breeder of these precious birds.

Support the baby's body and feet in your cupped hands when removing him for feeding. Using too firm a grasp when picking up

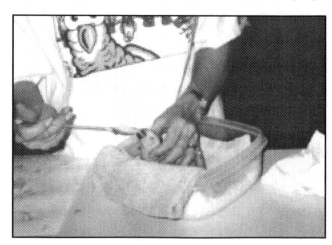

the baby with the palm across the back and the fingers on the abdomen can cause bruising of the internal organs. The baby will kick and squirm because he doesn't feel safe when he is picked up in the manner described above.

Loosely make a circle of your thumb and middle finger to support the baby under the jaws as he eats. Cup your palm over the baby's shoulders during feeding for additional warmth if he is unfeathered. A heat lamp at a SAFE distance can also be used for warmth. A cloth padded container makes a safe and comfortable place for the baby during feeding. The babies can dig their dagger-point toenails into the cloth diaper—paper towels are too slippery.

After you finish feeding, wipe the beak clean with a very warm damp paper towel. If the baby resists the beak wiping, lean in close and softly reassure him. Carefully wipe first one side of the beak, then the other and then the bottom beak. One should never touch or hold the beak of a feeding baby or put any pressure on the beak when wiping it clean. The babies' beaks can suffer compression deformities or lateral deviation of the beak when pressure is exerted on it feeding after feeding, day after day.

When you return the baby to the brooder, cup him in your hands, his backside toward you so that there is no pressure on his full crop. Allow the baby to fully position himself in his "nest" before you remove your hands. This extra carefulness will pay dividends at a much later time—the babies will feel safe and secure with humans. This is one of the early first steps toward a self-confident and trusting Grey.

Socializing for Bold Babies Begins at Once

Hang brightly colored moving toys in the babies' brooder so they will come to realize

that color and movement is safe. When they are old enough to nibble at the weaning foods, put some small toys on the floor of the brooder—plastic cat toys are small enough for the babies to move around and try to kill. Relocate the brooder at least twice so the babies are accustomed to change from the earliest weeks of life.

Multiple babies can be housed in at least two and sometimes three different cages in different locations with different toys. The different cages, locations, and toys accustom the babies to change and variety. As a consequence, when a baby goes to his new home - it's "Oh, well..... another new cage." The baby who is accustomed to change won't miss a beat digging into his food dishes in his new cage. I had one new owner thank me for selling him a "bird butt". He said that was all he saw of his bird for the first two weeks. He brought her back to be weighed and she had gained 30 grams in two weeks.

The babies may not recognize you in different colored clothing or with a new hair cut or style or they are startled because baby birds startle easily. Begin from the first day making a soft clucking sound. They may not know it's you but they come to recognize the sound. This clucking noise is one of the first sounds the babies make - they have heard it so frequently and it is associated with pleasant things happening. A startled clutch of Grey babies are growling gray puff balls.

Monitoring Babies' Weights - The Essential Measure of Health

Weigh the babies each morning on an empty crop. While weight charts offer a very general guideline, differences in formula and handfeeding technique as well as other variables, can combine to give the handfeeder a false sense of security.

A more accurate way to gauge the progress of the baby is to use the percentage of body weight gained in a 24 hour period—from morning to morning. Subtract the weight on the morning of the previous day from the weight on the morning of the current day.

To determine the percentage, the 24 hour gain is divided by the weight on the morning of the previous day and multiplied by 100. For example: if the baby weighed 13.58 grams on Monday morning and weighed 16.18 on Tuesday morning, he gained 2.6 grams during the 24 hour period from Monday morning to Tuesday morning. Divide the gain of 2.6 grams by 13.58 and multiply by 100. The percent of body weight gain is rounded to 19%. Young babies should gain a much greater percentage than older babies–typically 15%-25%.

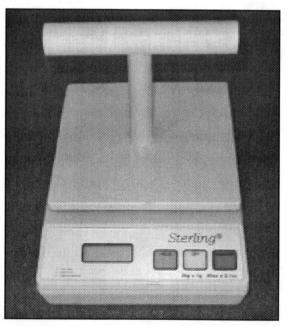

Gram scales are the best way to monitor your babies' weight gains. Most scales also come with a bowl.

A more typical daily gain pattern: a Grey baby weighed 146.1 on Monday morning and 163.4 grams on Tuesday morning; the 24 hour gain is 17.3 grams. The gain of 17.3 grams is divided by the 146.1 weight, and multiplied by 100. This calculates out rounded to 11.8%.

Whether a gain is good or inadequate depends on the weight and the age of the baby. A five gram gain on a 25 gram baby is 20% while a five gram gain on a 100 gram baby is only 5%. Using the percent of body weight gained method will give the handfeeder a much better picture of how the baby is gaining. You may find that you often get a good percentage on an older baby (12%-15%) on one day and a smaller percentage (8%-10%) the following day. It appears that the "off" day is a resting period for the body. As the babies get older, the percentages may drop to a range of 3%-7%. The baby should gain weight every day until he begins refusing formula and weaning weight losses begin. Handfeeders and babies are individuals and weight gains will vary. The active baby, the cold baby, the hot baby, the sick baby, the dehydrated baby, the poor eater, the regurgitating baby will gain less well than the one who just eats, sleeps, and poops in comfort.

The quality of baby formula is related to weight gain, therefore it is very important to buy the freshest commercial formula possible. If the formula is old or has been stored improperly a baby's health can be seriously compromised, he can fail to thrive or gain adequately. Always check for an expiration date or the date of manufacture and buy the freshest formula. Some companies use the Julian code to date their products. The first three digits are the day of the year, the fourth digit indicates the year. For example: 0039 means the formula was manufactured on January 3, 1999. Sometimes a letter will be added (0039K) but it is meaningless as far as date of manufacture is concerned.

Weaning Strategies

Babies on a 8am, 12pm, 4pm, 8pm, and 12am handfeeding schedule will have good weight gains until they begin to refuse formula at around ten weeks of age. The first feeding to drop is the 12pm feeding; then drop the 8pm feeding. The 8am and the midnight feedings are the last to go. Soaked warm Zupreem Primate Biscuits can be substituted for the morning feeding if the babies are only losing the few grams a day. Add a feeding back in if the weight loss is more than expected. Weaning is a dynamic rather than a rigid process with the bird as your guide. Expect that one step forward will be accompanied by an occasional two steps back to cater to the individual baby's emotional and physical needs. Weaning is a process, a long process, not an event.

My Grey babies will, on average, lose around 30 grams from their peak weight at around 10 weeks. This can be attributed to the very early introduction of weaning foods. When the oldest baby begins picking at his band, his toes, his clutch mates' toes, the poops, or the design on a receiving blanket, put the weaning foods in the brooder. This usually happens around 5-6 weeks old.

Place a wide shallow light colored bowl and a few small pieces of brightly colored fruits and veggies along with a small portion

birdie bread and a teaspoon of a bean/grains mixture. Use several of the following cut into very small pieces: an apple with the peel left on, a square of cooked carrot, a green pea, sprouts (the pink lentils are very eye catching), a quartered red or white grape, a blueberry or a cranberry cut in half. In an effort to ensure that the babies are successful nibbling on the weaning foods, very small pieces are offered. They can pin the food down either in the bowl or on the floor of the brooder and nibble on it. If you scatter food on the brooder floor, the babies may pick at the high contrast poops thinking these are just another weaning food. At this time, remove the poop frequently so the babies don't have access to it.

Use another bowl for the crunchy foods. Offer several different kinds of small pellets and add a few Cherrios and a couple of Multi-Grain Chex. These foods are easy for the babies to bite into. If the babies have to struggle with foods that are difficult to eat or to bite into, they will get discouraged. The littlest ones, who can barely waddle around, will have their beaks coated with birdie bread. The oldest chick will lead the way.

The youngest babies proceed at an accelerated rate due to the example of eating the weaning foods set by the older birds. The youngest baby in a clutch will wean earlier than one would expect. Timely weaning indicates a healthy bird—both physically and psychologically.

When they are a little older, begin to add larger size pellets. Give a bowl of fresh soft foods after each handfeeding except after the midnight feeding. When the babies have a full crop, they are more willing to explore the weaning foods. Eating the weaning foods is a natural and normal activity for weaning babies because of this very early introduction. The transition from handfeeding to eating on their own is an easy one. By offering very warm pieces of soaked primate biscuit as a substitute for a feeding, a baby can sometimes go from two feedings a day to none in the space of a day or two. The babies will eat four or five bowls of soft and crunchy weaning foods and several soaked primate biscuits a day—they are too full to hold formula too.

Encourage the new owners and responsible others in the home to continue feeding a very warm soaked primate biscuit or other soft warm foods several times a week. Feeding by hand is pleasurable for both the bird and the owners. It is also a useful way to include others who are not the bird's special person. A Grey need never be a one-person bird. Life will be more interesting for the bird if he has a whole "flock" of humans with whom to interact.

A young weaned Grey should be fed a breeder formulation pellet until he is one year old. The breeder pellet has higher protein, higher fat, and more calories than the maintenance pellet. The youngster will have to put back on the weight lost during weaning. The breeder pellet will also prepare the body for the first molt which occurs at around 8 months.

Weaning is one of the most important times in a Grey's life–make it as stress free as possible for him. If you will make food available early and in abundance, attractively presented and interesting, you will have an easy time with your weaning babies. Most importantly, the baby will not feel starved and will not come to see you as the cause of his starvation. Forced weaned baby birds cannot feel safe. Therefore, they are behaving predictably when they act fearfully and suspicious of humans. Intended or not, the lesson learned by a forced weaned baby is very clear: He cannot rely on the very per-

son whom the baby is totally dependent upon to meet his most basic needs. Forced weaning is crazy making and can result in the following life-long distressed behaviors:

- picky eating
- chronic begging
- food phobias
- a distrust of humans
- loud vocalizing or calling
- separation anxiety
- plucking or feather chewing from stress
- excessive digging
- agitated nipping or pinching

Babies are individuals and should be allowed to wean at their own rate. A successful weaning schedule is one in which the baby never feels deprived and always feels safe, cared for, and loved.

The Weaning Cage and Advanced Socialization

When the babies are mostly feathered, they can be introduced to the weaning cage. The Midwest 24x19x20 crate has a full size door that is very convenient and has ample interior room for a clutch. Begin by leaving the mostly feathered babies in the weaning cage for an hour and gradually increase the time over a week or so until you feel they will be comfortable and warm spending their first night in the weaning cage.

Begin with a natural branch laying on the floor of the cage. As the babies become more and more coordinated, raise the perch up to the first vertical bar that is about 6 inches from the bottom of the cage. Leave the food bowls on the floor of the cage and put the water in put in a cup and hanger so it won't get tipped over. Remove the water cup after the midnight feeding. Water drinking is a learned behavior; watch the babies very closely to make sure they are drinking. Give them soft foods four or five times a day. Put many toys in the cage so they aren't fearful of toys when they go to their new homes. The new owners should continue to expose them to new toys.

Touch and kiss the babies a lot. You can put your whole head inside the cage and kiss nearby body parts. Position the weaning cage on the kitchen countertop or on a stand where the most activity takes place. They will soon become accustomed to movement and commotion. Speak to them and interact with them many, many times a day. By the time they are in the weaning cage, they should be accustomed to being kissed and touched. Place your hands on either side of the birds' body under the wings and kiss them on the back between the wings; lift one wing at a time and kiss the side of the body.

They have long before this time welcomed full body petting—from head to tail. Some babies love to have the bare area under the bottom beak kissed. Hold the head loosely (palm on the top of the head) and kiss the sides of the beak or the top curve of the beak. Demonstrate the handling, kissing, and cuddling to the new owners if they are local so they will have an idea of what the babies expect and will accept. Selling early and locally gives you more time to get to know the new owners and more time to educate them. The new owners get to practice the handling, the cuddling, the soft coaxing tones, the slow movements, the offering of toys and foods. They will enjoy feeding the babies the small pieces of food by hand.

The Importance of Flight

Allow the babies to fly until they have learned to control their flight, can land where they intend to, and can land on the floor safely. Drapes or blinds on windows and patio doors should be closed until the babies learn they are solid. It can get a little wild with babies landing on your head, on the edge of the newspaper, and various other places that won't hold their weight. Watching two fledglings trying to land on a lampshade at the same time can be quite amusing. Allowing them to fledge helps enormously with the weaning process. If they are never allowed to fly, they will be clumsy, anxious, and insecure. Bred into the bones is the notion that birds fly—that's what birds do—they fly. They want to fly so badly that they cannot concentrate on eating until they are proficient flyers. Eating is not nearly as much fun as flying. Being able to do both makes for a self-confident, independent, well-adjusted bird.

Before Your Babies Leave Your Care

Keep the baby for seven to ten days after he is fully weaned. The blood calcium test results will be invalid if the baby is still on the handfeeding formula that contains the calcium required for growth and health. He should be eating on his own and maintaining his weight. The routine pre-purchase health exam covers: Gram's stain, Complete Blood Count, blood calcium level test, and the PBFD screen. DNA sexing, polyoma-virus vaccination and micro-chipping are much appreciated by the new owner. I have never had a Grey baby who required a daily calcium supplementation but it does happen. If a bird needs daily calcium supplementation, it does not mean the bird is unhealthy or will suffer from ill health in the future. It is very important the new owner understand that a blood calcium level test should be run at each annual exam.

Don't risk the life or psychological well being of a Grey baby by selling him unweaned. It doesn't take a rocket scientist to handfeed but subtle signs of illness or dysfunction may be missed by the novice handfeeder. Leaving aside the very real dangers of aspiration, underfeeding, and crop burns experienced by some babies in the hands of novices, breeders who sell only weaned babies have light years more experience in properly weaning and socializing a baby Grey than does the retail client. Don't devalue your knowledge, skill, and talent by letting an unprofessional finish your work raising a healthy, well-adjusted baby.

How can you be sure the baby will stay in the home you have chosen for him if you leave the weaning and socializing to a retail client? Greys are the most vulnerable and sensitive of birds and they need careful, aware, and considerate socialization techniques. Greys are thought of by some as cage-bound, plucking, shy, one-person birds. This need never be true. A Grey baby should be assertive, unafraid, adventurous and curious.

Take the time to make sure the babies are successful; encourage independence and exploration; expose them to many new safe experiences; accustom them to variety, movement, new locations, and normal household activity. The old canard that a bird must be fed by the owner to establish a bond is an idea whose time has long passed. A trusting, well adjusted, properly socialized bird will quickly adapt to the new owner, although sometimes the adjustment can take longer than the normal three weeks. A well-socialized baby bird expects only good times with humans - and why not? All of his experiences so far have been pleasant ones.

Educate the Buyer

The importance of a varied diet is an area of care that should be extensively discussed with the buyer. Feeding Your Pet Bird (ISBN 0-8120-1521-5) published by Barron's and authored by Petra Burgmann DVM, is an excellent book to offer as a part of the purchase price or for sale to the buyer. Consider printing a pamphlet that covers diet, cages, household dangers, toys, recipes for "birdie bread" and the beans/grains mix, as well as health and care information for the new owner.

Recommend organic human-grade foods for the bird; ask the buyer to consider feeding organic Harrison's Bird Diet. The babies will be accustomed to eating several different pellets and should accept almost any pellet. The maintenance pellet for the juvenile and adult years should be in the lower protein range.

Strongly encourage local buyers to visit as frequently as possible before the baby is weaned. Encourage them to delay choosing a particular baby for as long as possible; give yourself as much time as possible to determine which baby would be best in their home. Birds are such complex animals and psychologically evolve in complex ways as personality begins to form and develop. Invite the local owners to accompany you to the vet's office. Encourage them to ask questions of the vet and to open an account at the clinic so they will receive an annual notice that the health check is due. Should the baby have a low blood calcium level, the avian vet can instruct the owners how to supplement the bird.

Sell your babies to someone you would want as a friend. Interview the buyers carefully before you accept a deposit for a baby. After the baby leaves, keep in touch to make sure that all is going well.

The Egg

When a hen ovulates, the egg erupts from the surface of the ovary and "falls" into the funnel shaped upper reaches of the reproductive system where fertilization takes place. Transit time through the reproductive system can take up to 24 hours, depending on species.

As the egg travels through the reproductive system, various components are added:

A table showing egg development until hatching as well as normal and difficult hatches is found at the end of this article.

• First, the membrane layers surrounding the yolk are laid down. The yolk provides nutrition for the growing embryo and contains maternal antibodies. The membranes protect the embryo from microorganisms.

• Next, important internal structures for stabilizing and centering the yolk, the chalazae, are added. The chalazae are composed of thick strands of twisted albumen. It attaches to the inner shell membrane at the blunt end of the egg (the air cell end), to the inner shell membrane at the small end of the egg, and surrounds the yolk.

• Next, the layers of albumen (the clear viscous fluid of the egg), along with sodium, magnesium and calcium, are added. The albumen provides the embryo with nutrition and protection from microorganisms.

• Next, the inner and outer shell membranes are added. These membranes function as a transpiration medium (oxygen and carbon dioxide waste exchange) and protect the embryo from microorganisms.

• Next, the formation of the cuticle (the shell of the egg) is initiated. The cuticle provides physical protection, facilitates the exchange of oxygen through microscopic pores in the shell, and regulates evaporation.

• Next, water is added.

• Finally, the egg is in position (small end out first) and is ready to be layed.

Eggs lose weight during incubation. The daily weight loss, which varies by species, is very small and measured in hundredths of a gram. For example: 0.012 grams to 0.017 grams might be a normal daily egg weight loss for the eggs of some larger species. The eggs of the various species have a range of desirable weight loss – minimum and maximum. The range can vary dramatically from species to species. Some larger species' eggs lose as little as 12% of the fresh layed weight; some as much as 20% of the fresh layed weight.

Weight loss is largely governed by the relative humidity in the egg incubator machine during artificial incubation. If the egg loses too much weight, the baby can be dehydrated at hatch. Dehydrated babies usually stick to the membranes and often have to be assisted to hatch. This is called a "dry hatch". If the egg loses too little, the baby's tissues can be fluid-filled at hatch. This is called a "wet hatch". Avoiding both conditions is sometimes difficult in artificial incubation.

An artificially incubated egg will often develop faster and hatch closer to the normal range of incubation-to-hatch than will a parent incubated egg. The temperature is constant in the egg incubator, unlike under the hen. There is no "cooling off" or "period of inattention" in the incubator as there is when the hen leaves the eggs for short periods during incubation. A typical incubation-to-hatch range would be 26-28 days for some of the larger psittacines.

A candler is a small focused light source, similar to a Mag flashlight. Most often it will have an extended hood that fits closely on the surface of the egg. Eggs are candled

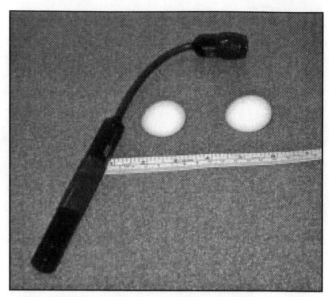

A candler is useful to determine whether an egg is fertile as well as monitor, the progress of a developing embryos.

from the air cell end of the egg in a dark room. The light illuminates the interior of the egg; the detail that can be seen is quite remarkable.

The Hatching Egg

To illustrate the following explanation, I have included a diary at the end of this section detailing the hatching process for three eggs. The first was an uneventful hatch; the other two were difficult ones. Since most non-breeders know little about the hatching process, these diary entries may be of interest.

The hatcher is a unit maintained at 1 degree F less than the egg incubation temperature. Relative humidity in the hatcher was 65%-70%+ during the process. High humidity is necessary to prevent the inner shell membranes from sticking to the body, head, or beak of the baby. If the baby sticks, he will be unable to rotate inside the egg to make consecutive external pips to free himself from the egg. The observations of

the hatching eggs were made with a candler.

The air cell is in the blunt end of the egg and is between the inner shell membrane and the outer shell membrane, which separate to form the air cell. The air cell is where the baby breaks through to oxygen at the beginning of the hatching process and begins the transition from fluid to air breathing. This is called "internal pip".

There will be a slight rippling at the air cell line as the baby begins to push against the membrane that separates him from oxygen. The first sign that internal pip is approaching is a drop in the position of the air cell line. When the membrane of the air cell is pierced, the air cell line will drop dramatically from its original position. This is called "drawdown". The baby will puncture this membrane; access the oxygen he needs to dry the moisture out of the respiratory tract and become air breathing. The drying-out of the respiratory tract will be accompanied by sticking or crackling sounds as the walls of the respiratory tract touch and separate from one another as oxygen is inhaled and exhaled.

The baby will move up into the air cell and begin using his egg tooth to tap against the inner surface of the eggshell. The egg tooth is located on the upper end portion of the upper beak. In some babies who take a very long time to hatch or who are exceptionally vigorous, the egg tooth will be blunted and worn down from friction. Some species, without pigmentation of the beak at hatch, will have hemorrhage or bruising under the surface of the soft keratin of the beak if the hatch is prolonged or difficult. Grey babies hatch with black beaks and black toenails on their pink feet.

The baby's body will contract and release, contract and release as he bangs his egg tooth against the shell. Good rhythmic contractions indicate that a baby is strong and working hard to hatch. Babies have a large hatching muscle on the back of the neck. This muscle shrinks to normal size in the days following hatch.

The baby will bang away continuously for days, depending on species, until an external hole is made in the eggshell. This is called "external pip". The baby will peep almost continually as he taps away at the inner surface of the eggshell. Some babies are so vigorous, the egg will actually rock. An egg is constructed so that it is relatively easy to fracture it from the inside while requiring considerable force to fracture it from the outside.

The baby will work his way around the circumference of the egg at or very near the air cell line. The first external pip is to the right of center at the air cell line if the egg is held with the blunt end away from you. Each succeeding external pip is to the right of the first pip mark until the baby meets the original pip site and the top of the egg falls away. The baby will brace his feet in the lower portion of the egg to push himself from the eggshell; sometimes wearing the cut off top of the eggshell like a hat.

If the baby isn't strong or if the eggshell is too thick, the area where the baby is attempting to pip can be lightly sanded to help the baby break through. It is clear where this area is because you can see the baby hitting the inside of the eggshell when you candle the egg. Also, as he wears away the inner surface of the eggshell by hitting on it, this area will be lighter than the surrounding area. If the baby hasn't made the first external pip approximately 24+ hours after he is air breathing, he will require oxygen from the outside if he is to survive. The air cell's supply of oxygen is limited. A small pinhole is made, very carefully so as not to injure the baby, at the very top of the egg air cell to allow oxygen to enter.

At hatch, the only remaining structure that connects him to the egg is a large umbilicus vein at his "belly button". This vein will usually have a blood supply still in it and must be carefully cut with a sterile instrument about an inch away from the baby's body. The vein will dry up and fall away in a few days.

These observations are from the eggs and babies of one pair and don't necessarily indicate the "norm" or the average. Others may manage their hatching eggs in dramatically different ways.

Daily Development (Day Zero = 5/2/91)

Day 0	The egg is layed.
Day 1	Rosy-yellow tone to yolk.
Day 2	No change.
Day 3	Very small slightly red dot in yolk; yolk thicker, moves slower upon rotation; slightly opaque.
Day 4	No change.
Day 5	It's a baby! Heartbeat! Small red dot; beginning of veins.
Day 6	Veins more developed; some veins up to the air cell but mostly in yolk area; dot is more diffuse.
Day 7	Dot is very red; more veins up to air cell line; dot is very fuzzy in shape.
Day 8	Dot is larger; veins 2/3 around egg.
Day 9	Veins are mostly in the yolk area; veins are very red and extensive.
Day 10	Veins very red.
Day 11	Veins very red; filling out the lower portion of the egg. Movement!
Day 12	Egg encased in veins; baby very vigorous.
Day 13	Veins all around, a little thin; baby moving around very vigorously.
Day 14	No movement, veins still good and red.
Day 15	Good movement.
Day 16	Good movement; good veins; air cell is a good size.
Day 17	Very good movement; veins strong and very red. Baby is kicking his feet!
Day 18	Baby is darker; veins red; slight movement; air cell is good.
Day 19	Veins strong; good movement.
Day 20	Same as day 19; very positive appearance.
Day 21	Egg darker; very good movement.
Day 22	Ripple at air cell line; not much movement.
Day 23	Quiet movement; expanded air cell.
Day 24	Slight slant in air cell line; egg very dark; baby pushing against air cell line.
Day 25	Very steep slant in air cell line; put egg into hatcher at maximum humidity; rippling of air cell line; not real active; 10pm heard peeping. He's air breathing!
Day 26	Baby is tapping and peeping in the air cell; working on external pip at 12pm.
Day 27	First and second external pip between 12:20am and 7:15am. Third external pip at 12pm. Baby is half way around at air cell line at 12:30pm. Hatched at 1:05pm. Weight: 14.8 grams.

An uneventful hatch: Egg Layed 8/27/91

9/19/91 DAY 23
9am - very slight dip in air cell line
(egg incubator observation)

9/20/91 DAY 24
9am - slightly lower dip in air cell line
(egg incubator observation)

9/21/91 DAY 25
9am, 12pm & 6pm – very close to drawdown
(egg incubator observation)
8pm – drawdown, egg put into hatcher

9/22/91 DAY 26
1pm – rippling at air cell line
5pm – crackling sounds, small tent in membrane at 6
o'clock position
7pm – shadows moving in air cell, very faint tapping
8pm – peeping, air breathing!
9pm – peeping & moving around 11pm - tapping

9/23/91 DAY 27
10:45am & 1pm – tapping
4:15pm – tapping & peeping
6pm to 8pm – first external pip

9/24/91 DAY 28
8am – hatched, weight 13.37 grams

A difficult hatch: Egg layed 1/12/92

2/4/92 DAY 23
9am & 3pm - dip in air cell line
(egg incubator observation)
4:40pm – put egg into hatcher
11pm – not complete drawdown, movement

2/5/92 DAY 24
12:15am – deeper drop in air cell line but not
complete drawdown
2:30am & 5am – activity on bottom side of egg
9:30am – activity on bottom side of egg, crackling
sounds
7:30pm & 9pm – shadows moving in air cell, tapping
11:15pm – lots of shadows moving in air cell,
  occasional tap

2/6/92 DAY 25
12am – movement on bottom side of egg
2:45am, 5am, 9:15am & 11am – some movement in
air cell 3pm – tapping
4pm – tapping, contractions, peeped!
5pm – tapping, contractions regular but not strong
2/6/92 DAY 25 (continued)
6pm – tapping & peeping (a LOT), unorganized
contractions, baby is not happy
7:45pm – tapping & peeping, contractions a
little stronger
10pm – tapping & peeping, contractions much stronger 11:30pm – tapping & peeping, shadows moving in
unusual places

2/7/92 DAY 26
2:20am – tapping & peeping, strong & regular
contractions
5am - tapping & peeping, flailing around, he wants OUT!
8am – tapping & peeping, made air hole, sanded area
where baby is tapping
10:30am, 11:30am & 2:15pm – tapping & peeping, sanded
a little wider area
3pm – contractions weaker
4:30pm – external pip, thank goodness!
7:30pm – baby enlarging original pip site, stuck?
9:45pm – assisted hatch, stuck, weight 12.32 grams

A difficult hatch: Egg Layed 1/17/94

2/8/94   DAY 22
9am – slight drop in air cell line
(egg incubator observation)

2/9/94   DAY 23
9am – slightly more of a drop in air cell line
(egg incubator observation)

2/10/94 DAY 24
9am – slightly deeper drop in air cell line
(egg incubator observation)

2/11/94 DAY 25
9am – almost drawdown (egg incubator observation)
2:30pm – put egg into hatcher
3:30pm & 4:30pm – no progress, not complete drawdown
7pm – deeper drop in air cell line, slight blurring
of air cell line on bottom of egg
9pm – movement on top & bottom of egg near air cell
line
11:30pm – deep drop in air cell line, full drawdown

2/12/94 DAY 26
5:30am – tapping & peeping
7am – first external pip
8am – baby changed position!
9:30am – occasional tap, mostly flailing around, head
under air cell membrane
10:45am – moving around, not much tapping
12pm – tapping & peeping, moving around
quite a lot
1:30pm – tapping but not rhythmic or strong
2:30pm – tapping a little steadier
4:30pm, 7:30pm & 10:30pm – tapping, contractions
steady but not strong

2/13/94 DAY 27
12:30am – moving around a LOT, peeping, contractions
a little stronger
3am - tapping & peeping, no progress, stuck?
5am – no more external pips, stuck!
8:15am – assisted hatch, well & truly stuck, weight 13.08
grams

Handfeeding Methods: Good Methods Yield Good Pets

Handfeeding, socialization, and weaning are the three most significant issues in raising a baby bird. They are so intertwined that it is almost impossible to separate the three. How a baby bird is handled at this time in his life will leave a lasting impression that will affect him for the rest of his life. It will make the difference between a healthy, trusting, well-behaved companion bird and a bird who is insecure, fearful, unsociable, and a poor eater.

In previous articles, I have discussed the importance of the proper methods of weaning and socialization and have explained the dangers of buying an unweaned bird. This article addresses the various techniques of handfeeding in an effort to help the pet owner ask appropriate questions of a qualified breeder or pet store. It is not intended to instruct potential pet owners in handfeeding techniques.

Purchase your weaned baby from a carefully selected breeder or pet store. A handfeeder who employs hands-on feeding techniques, a systematic socialization program, and weans bountifully can help guarantee your bird will become a well-loved and permanent member of your family.

Handfeeding is one of the early experiences through which a bird can learn trust in humans. But this will only occur if the proper handfeeding methods are used. Good handfeeding methods build upon the natural feeding instincts of the babies, creating comfortable, warm and confident feelings in them, and building their trust in humans. Good handfeeding methods also require time and care from the handfeeder.

Some feeding methods are detrimental to baby birds. These methods bypass the birds' natural feeding instincts in the interest of saving time. As a result, birds don't discover the taste of food or how to eat and may not be handled enough to be properly socialized. They may be sold as "handfed" birds, but they will not be the wonderful companion birds that their owners expect. They may, in fact, be less tame than if their parents had raised them because they weren't given adequate time for the socialization associated with early handfeeding.

Quality breeders and pet stores will use more time-consuming handfeeding methods, coupled with bountiful weaning. Those interested only in making a profit will use techniques that require less of their time. Many will force-wean a baby in order to sell it earlier. The problems that the bird and future pet owner may experience are of no concern to them.

When buying a bird, it is not enough to ask if a bird is handfed. Ask also what handfeeding methods were used. If you buy a bird that has been improperly handfed, socialized, or weaned, be prepared to spend the time and effort it will take to overcome problems that may have been created by improper care in his early life. Any ONE of these, when done improperly, could lead to problems.

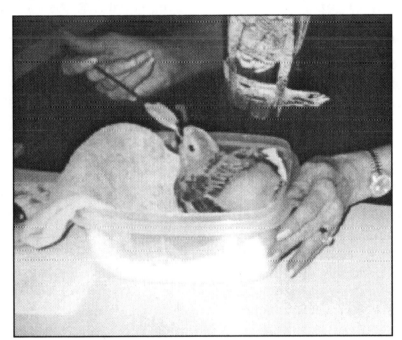

mula is easily controlled. The handfeeder can watch the baby closely; know when the mouth is full; and when the baby needs to draw a breath. The baby is fed with the spoon in an almost horizontal position.

It is very dangerous to put food into the mouth of a baby who has no feeding response. During a feeding response or "pumping," the opening to the trachea is closed and it is safe to feed so long as the baby is pumping and swallowing. With some species, like cockatoos, pressure against the inside tip of the upper beak will elicit a feeding response. With some other species, like Greys, very gently pushing the spoon into the mouth so that the formula is delivered at the back of the mouth will elicit a feeding response.

Spoon Feeding

Spoon feeding is the time-tested way to feed. It uses the baby's natural feeding response, teaches the bird how to eat, and introduces him to the taste of food.

Iced tea spoons (with the long handles) and the sides bent up to form a trough lend themselves to the shape of a baby bird's beak. There is no chance of pressure against the beak that could cause the beak to become misshapen; the flow of the for-

Some breeders use a Dixie cup with one edge pinched to a point. I've never used this method but it certainly sounds easy and there are no bowls to wash up after feeding.

Syringe Feeding

Syringe feeding is a widely used handfeeding technique. This method also uses the natural feeding response and teaches the baby how to eat. The handfeeder elicits the feeding response by touching the sides of the beak. The syringe is then inserted into the beak and pressure on the plunger of syringe is used to release the formula. The flow of the formula can be controlled, but the sight of the baby's mouth is somewhat obscured by the syringe and it is more difficult to know when the mouth is full. A major concern with the use of soft plastic syringes is the problem of safely disinfecting them.

Gavage Feeding

The bird's natural feeding response is bypassed using the gavage method. It involves inserting a feeding needle, or soft vein tubing threaded onto the end of a syringe, directly into the crop. The metal feeding needle can cause bruising of the esophagus unless inserted with extreme care. The soft vein tubing has a smooth round end with small openings for the formula to empty into the crop. The vein tubing is less traumatic to the esophagus than the metal feeding tube but must still be inserted very carefully.

It is difficult but possible for the tubing or the needle to be inserted into the trachea. If this is done, the bird will die from the formula going into the lungs. This is called aspiration.

Gavage feeding is typically used by handfeeders with too many babies to feed. Babies fed in this manner don't learn to eat and can be very difficult to wean. The baby is fed in a matter of seconds with little human contact. Some gavage handfeeders will give a little bit of formula into the mouth so that the baby will know the feeling of food in his mouth.

Gavage feeding has its place in the treatment of birds that are too ill to feed themselves, or with sick babies who have lost the feeding response. These are the only circumstances in which it should be used. It is important to ask the handfeeder before buying a baby bird if his babies are gavage fed.

Power Feeding

A technique called "power feeding," which employs a syringe and which is a very quick way to handfeed, is often used. After a feeding response is elicited, the syringe contents are quickly emptied into the bird's esophagus. The force of the formula being ejected from the syringe keeps the esophagus open and the trachea closed. The whole contents of the syringe can be delivered in seconds. It is similar to gavage feeding, in that the food bypasses the mouth. The baby does not learn the taste of food or how to eat.

Power feeding is a method employed by handfeeders who have many babies to feed. Avoid purchasing a bird that has been fed in this manner unless you can determine that this method was used only so that the handfeeder would have adequate time to socialize many babies. Bountiful weaning and intensive socialization are critical to the baby's development if power feeding is employed.

Power and gavage feeding are one of the *triple threats* to the production of a calm, tame, trusting companion bird—inadequate socialization and forced weaning are the other two.

Buy a weaned baby bird that was handfed properly, weaned bountifully, and intensively socialized. If the seller doesn't do these things, find one who will.

Handfeeding Parrots: Cornerstone to A Good Pet Bird

Anyone who purchases a bird wants a companion who can share and enrich his life. We want a bird that is healthy, trusting, sociable, fun, and affectionate. A bird who will be a positive addition to our family, bringing us joy and happiness and receiving the same in return. Birds are very long lived and you can expect your new companion to be with you for a very long time. So take the time to pick the right bird and the right breeder.

A baby bird's experiences in the first few months of his life affect him for the rest of his days. Proper methods of handfeeding, weaning, and socialization make the difference between a healthy, trusting, well behaved companion bird and a bird who is insecure, fearful, unsociable, and a poor eater . Before you purchase a bird, be sure to ask questions about how the bird was raised. And never buy an unweaned bird.

Many people have been told that the bond between bird and owner will be deeper if the pet owner handfeeds his bird. This is not true. A deeper bond may occur on the part of the owner, but the disadvantages and the risks are too great. A mature and educated buyer will have no problem bonding with a tame, responsive, weaned baby bird. A baby bird can and will bond to a human he trusts after the weaning period. Many birds have bonded with second and third owners.

Why Hand Feed A Bird

Handfeeding a baby bird takes a great deal of time and effort. It is much easier to allow the parent birds to feed the babies. In addition, parent-fed babies are bigger than babies who are hand fed from a young age or from day one. So why handfeed?

Handfeeding accustoms baby birds to human contact. The handfeeder takes on the parents' role of feeding the baby. In this way, humans come to be perceived as part of the flock and the baby becomes accustomed to being touched and to the sound of the human voice. Adult birds, like humans, are the product of their early socialization. A baby who learns to trust humans in the early weeks and months of life will make an excellent companion bird.

The handfeeding process begins at about two or three weeks and continues until the baby is completely weaned. Many breeders take the baby birds from the parents when the oldest is two or three weeks old. This enables the chicks to get the benefit of parental feeding when they are smallest and most vulnerable. It also minimizes the risks of handfeeding a very young, small bird. There is still sufficient time for the baby to be well socialized and hand tamed.

The Dangers of Buying an Unweaned Bird

Many sellers convince novice buyers to take an unweaned bird. Some even offer a discount. This is money you do not want to save. If something goes wrong, will you know what to do? Some sellers will help if the pet owner needs help, but some won't. Can you tell who will and who won't when you leave with an unweaned bird?

The act of handfeeding isn't too complex for an inexperienced person to learn. When everything goes well and the inexperienced handfeeder does all he has been told to do, handfeeding isn't such a big deal. The really big deal occurs when things don't go well. A problem that is a red flag to the experienced handfeeder may go unrecognized by the inexperienced handfeeder until it is too late.

Many baby birds do well in less than ideal circumstances. However, the emotional and financial investment is so great that a buyer must ask himself: Is it worth taking the chance that everything will go well? A whole host of problems await the novice handfeeder. Breeders and handfeeders have gained experience in how to handle them and prevent sick, stunted, injured, or dead babies.

• Signs of trouble - Lack of feeding response, respiratory sounds, slight aspiration, delayed crop emptying, restless or lethargic babies, and lack of weight gain are just a few symptoms of trouble. These indicators require prompt action if the baby is to be saved. With babies in trouble, the first system that shuts down is the digestive system. Very close attention must be paid to the slightest clue that the digestive system is not performing as it should.

Lack of proper weight gain is an important signal of trouble. An experienced person knows how much weight gain to expect. If a baby is not gaining weight as he should, he may need more frequent feedings or a different formula. Or this may be indicative of serious problems.

• Crop burn - Improperly heated formula can have hot spots. Babies will eat scalding hot formula that can burn away the esophagus and/or the crop. If the burn is very serious, the baby will die. Implanting a feeding tube in the crop can save some burned babies, but the esophagus must be intact for the bird to live after the tube is removed.

Some crop burns will make a fistula to the outside of the body. If the burned area is small, the baby often can be saved by cutting away the dead crop area and stitching it together, leaving a smaller but functional crop. This has to be watched very carefully by an avian vet as the flesh often continues to die.

• Crop stasis - The temperature of the brooder and the formula are very important. Low temperatures can cause the crop to shut down. Unfeathered babies cannot regulate their body temperatures and don't have the reserves to heat cool or cold formula up to digestion temperature. When inappropriately cool formula is fed, the crop doesn't empty. Formula that sits in the warm environment of the crop can sour or become contaminated from the small number of impurities in the handfeeding formula. The formula powder is not sterile. Often the body will draw on the fluid in the formula to hydrate the body and the food can get compacted in the crop. Delayed emptying of the crop is very serious and needs immediate attention.

Bacterial, fungal, and yeast infections can also cause a crop to stop emptying. Everything that touches or is in contact with a baby must be clean. Babies pick up gram positive bacteria from the environment. The handfeeder's responsibility is to make sure they don't pick up gram negative bacteria, yeast or fungal spores. Babies don't have the reserves, or a fully competent immune system, to be able to ward off these contaminants.

• Aspiration - This occurs when large or small amounts of formula enter the baby's lungs. When the babies aren't given time to swallow or the mouth is flooded, aspiration is a real possibility. Care must be taken with the very liquid formula/water mixtures required by neonates. If a small amount of formula is aspirated, the baby may be saved by prompt competent medical treatment. If the amount of formula aspirated is significant, the baby will die immediately—there is no treatment.

• Beak Deformities - It is possible to cause a deviation unless careful attention is paid to avoid pressure of the feeding implement against the chick's beak. By far the more usual cause of lateral deviation or compression deformities occurs from faulty technique.

Applying too much pressure wiping the beak can cause it to deviate from true. Often one can see the indentations or compression deformities when a thumb and forefinger are used to clean the bottom beak.

• Poor socialization - The experienced handfeeder knows how important very early socialization is and will take care that the babies are kept warm, safe, and secure. A novice might think that because the babies are very young or blind, they aren't aware of the handling they receive. But they are—and at a younger age than one would ever think. Blind babies especially need a reassuring touch. They frighten easily. A gentle touch is required for all babies, but the very young are quite responsive to a soft voice and a tender hand.

• When and How to Wean - The experienced handfeeder watches very carefully for the first sign that the baby will respond to the weaning foods and is ready to begin the long process of weaning. Weaning is a process, not an event. There is a window of opportunity and age, around six weeks for the larger birds, when the baby will explore low heavy bowls of brightly colored or interesting foods. If the baby is accustomed to seeing food from a very early age, he will be drawn to the weaning foods naturally, without stress or fear. Early unforced weaning is the proper way to wean a bird. It relies on the natural instincts of the bird, promotes trust and security, and prevents food related behavioral problems such as chronic begging, picky eating, whining, restlessness, and insecurity. A properly weaned bird is calm, trusting, self-confident, and a good eater. He understands and responds appropriately to humans and to his environment.

The beginning of the weaning period varies widely among species. As a general rule, the smaller the species, the sooner they wean. The Timneh is one of the smaller birds that requires as long or longer to wean than his redtail Grey relative. All babies are individuals and wean slightly differently from each other, even from their clutchmates. If these differences aren't accommodated, the chick's behavior and demeanor can be adversely affected. A bird's suitability as a companion bird can be impaired by forcing him to wean before he is emotionally ready.

If this window is missed, the bird's attitude toward food, his emotional development and his natural progression to food-independence will be retarded. Dr. Branson Ritchie, well known avian vet and researcher, states that, "Early unforced weaning is a sign of a physically and emotionally healthy bird".

• Health Guarantee - The health of an unweaned bird can't be guaranteed. Most sellers of unweaned birds will give the buyer a short time to have the bird vet checked. But, some of the tests are meaningless when done on a baby still handfeeding. Test values for babies are significantly different than for adults—this makes the use of an avian vet even more important.

A baby must be 5-6 weeks old to be screened for PBFD. He must be 35-40 days old before the first shot of the vaccination for polyoma can be given. The screen and the vaccination can protect the buyer from an emotional and financial disaster.

Handfeeding, socialization and weaning leave a mark on a bird forever. They affect him the rest of his life. It is almost impossible to separate the three.

Buy a baby bird who was weaned bountifully and intensively socialized. If the seller won't do these things, find one who will. Buy your baby bird from a quality breeder or pet store. Don't accept less—you and your baby bird deserve the best.

Bountiful Weaning: Secret To A Happy Bird

I have been using a bountiful weaning concept combined with intensive socializing on my African Grey babies for many years. It is my belief these techniques are instrumental in producing babies that are well behaved, social, independent, curious, and unafraid. It is the encouragement of these desirable traits that enables birds to become good companions, resulting in happy birds and happy bird owners.

A bountiful weaning program and intensive socializing works for African Greys and I believe it will work for other species as well.

The way a bird is weaned can affect his personality and behavior for the rest of its life. For this reason, it is very important to the bird and the new owner to ensure that only the most effective weaning method is used.

A young bird is shaped by the varied circumstances he encounters as he is going through the weaning process. He is learning social behavior, flock relationships, food independence, and how to fly. He regards his handfeeder and others around him as his flock or family. These relationships are crucial. The young bird relies on his handfeeder for food and security. He is building trust in humans via his prime caregiver.

Anything that interferes with this development, such as improper weaning methods, lack of toys, food deprivation, or unsympathetic humans can seriously affect the young bird for the rest of its life. Improperly weaned birds will have problems in trusting hu-

mans, can develop poor eating habits, and may even become feather mutilators.

For this reason, anyone buying a bird should ask questions about the techniques used during weaning and should never buy an unweaned bird.

A handfeeder who deprives a baby of food in a misguided attempt to wean him is setting the bird up for behavioral problems that may manifest themselves at a later period. Early exploration of brightly colored and small manageable pieces of food begins with a baby who is not hungry. A baby who whose hunger is satisfied is one who is willing to investigate not only the weaning foods but toys too. A hungry anxious baby will think of only one thing—his hunger and the handfeeder who is depriving him of food. It will be difficult for him to become a trusting, confident companion. He may regard a human as someone who once starved him.

And his owner will have no idea of why his new companion is never satisfied, is fearful, and distrusts those who want to reassure and love and protect him.

Baby birds, especially Greys, are unforgiving when subjected to forced or deprivation weaning. All the old canards—cage bound, shy, nippy—stem from a handfeeder who has failed to appreciate the delicacy with which Grey babies must be handled, both physically and emotionally. The intelligence of the Grey, so splendid to behold, makes the youngsters very sensitive to unpleasant or dangerous experiences.

Forced or survival weaning is devastating to the babies. Its root is with a handfeeder who weans on a rigid schedule. Baby birds are very much individuals. Some are more confident naturally, independent of conscious encouragement by the handfeeder. Some babies are more dependent and need a little extra reassurance, an extra feeding for a longer time. Those handfeeders who believe that all babies who are "x" weeks old should be on "y" feedings a day and weaned by "z" weeks old are the ones who sell anxious, fearful, nervous birds who are suspicious of unfamiliar foods, cages, toys, locations, people. This kind of weaning makes for birds that view unusual events or new toys with a jaundiced eye because they haven't learned to trust. How can they trust if the person upon whom they depended for life itself has withdrawn food and is allowing them to starve? Surely this is the baby's take on the situation.

An enlightened handfeeder will employ bountiful weaning. Bountiful weaning will produce a calm, trusting, confident youngster—a baby who expects only good things to happen. New toys are attacked vigorously; a new food immediately draws their attention; they will accept handling from strangers and from the new owner.

In a conscientiously applied program of bountiful weaning, babies are not allowed to go hungry. Nothing must interfere with the development of the baby. He must at all times feel safe and secure. Food in one form or another is offered often by the handfeeder. If the baby will only eat a small amount of formula, he still has a bowl of soft attractive soft foods in front of him. He is surrounded by food constantly and offered morsels of hot wet foods during and prior to weaning.

All of my babies are offered food very early. When you see a baby begin picking at his feet, his sibling's feet, or an imaginary spot on the brooder wall, you know he is ready for the weaning foods. This is usually around 6 weeks old although I have had the youngest of a large clutch begin exploring earlier because of the example set by an older chick. Begin with very small pellets, usually cockatiel size, because the smaller pellets allow the baby to be successful. The small pellets are easy to break and much more manageable for the clumsy babies. Add cereals such Cheerios and Chex; anything that is easy to eat or break apart.

Next offer a low, light colored, heavy crock of very small pieces of apple, orange, a grape cut into eighths, a small portion of a beans/rice mix, and a little crumbled up birdie bread. Brightly colored foods will draw their attention and the different taste sensations will interest and intrigue the babies. The weaning foods will show up better against a light background. Babies who are still holding up their toes when they walk will waddle around with their beaks covered with birdie bread.....a sight to warm the heart. Even after a full feeding, the babies will go directly to the crocks of food. Later in the weaning process, the formula is mostly for reassurance.

The babies, before and after fledging, will seldom eat as much as I would like and they lose weight. With a bountiful weaning program, I have been able to hold the weight losses to a minimum. Most lose 30 grams, but I have had stubborn babies who lost more. These are the headstrong individuals who try to wean themselves early. There is nothing to be done except try to make the weaning foods as attractive as possible. It's very dangerous to try to feed an unwilling bird. Aspiration is a real concern in this situation.

Sometimes I will have a sweeter, more dependent chick and continuing to handfeed him beyond the average weaning time will help with his self-confidence and independence. Sound contradictory? Not at all. Continuing a pleasant, fulfilling interaction (feeding) will help the baby be more confident if he knows that food is always available. The baby has options—we all gain self-confidence when we have options; and the luxury of not selecting the mature option but instead allowing another to indulge us out of love and kindness reassures the baby that food and attention and love and kindness will always be available to him.

In order for a buyer to reassure himself, he might ask a few questions of the handfeeder. First, to get an idea of how the handfeeder views the weaning process, a buyer might ask "When do your babies wean?" The answer should be "Babies are individuals and wean on a individual basis. I can't say for sure when a particular baby will wean."

Sally Blanchard published the best set of questions for the buyer to ask in the Pet Bird Report:

1. Can you provide me with references?

2. What do you want to know about me?

3. Tell me about your guarantee?

4. Tell me about the care and condition of the parent birds?

5. Do you sell unweaned babies?

6. At what age do you wean your babies?

7. Do you routinely gavage (tube) feed your babies?

8. What foods do you wean your baby parrots to?

9. How many babies do you raise at one time?

10. How do you socialize your babies?

11. How much individual attention do you give your babies?

12. Can you help me keep my baby a good pet?

Commonsense responses to commonsense questions will reassure you that you are buying from a quality breeder. A quality breeder will have his own set of questions to ask. A quality breeder cares where his baby bird is going; what the environment is like; whether there are children; whether there are other companion animals; whether the buyer has experience with birds; what the typical working hours are; whether the family is complete; what the social life is like; whether both the husband and wife want the bird. These are the kinds of questions a quality breeder will ask.

If all handfeeders used a bountiful weaning program, there would be fewer birds that needed rescuing. Fewer birds who were abused or neglected. Fewer birds who were naked, screaming, and isolated. How can it not be a better world when a bird has one permanent home and is a calm, trusting, well-behaved, and well-loved member of the family?

Interview the breeder extensively. Choose the breeder very carefully. Your bird will likely outlive you. It's very important to buy a baby bird that has had the very best start in life—one who will step up into your heart as quickly as your hand.

Living With Greys: All Things Considered

With this article, a big net was cast to collect many of the questions and concerns expressed by new Grey owners in their attempt to understand their beloved bird's behavior and to provide for his care. A dizzying array of topics is discussed ranging from airlines to zinc. The result is a sort of "starter kit" of considerations and information loosely organized into overlapping sections such as Normal Behavior and In Good Health.

So much is yet unknown regarding the behavior and needs of companion parrots. Still, the collective experience of those most deeply committed to companion birds has developed into a sound knowledge base from which the new bird owner can draw. Many of the topics discussed only briefly here have been written about in-depth in other publications. Find them. Never stop observing your bird's behavior analytically and searching for explanations and answers: You have a responsibility to your bird to become the most informed parent you can be. An open mind, careful observation, and an unfailingly gentle touch will serve your bird well as you become more experienced.

Normal Behavior In Grey Birds

Many of the normal actions of our Greys are especially puzzling or worrisome when viewed from the new or single bird owner's perspective. It is interesting to consider that

some of the behaviors we have come to accept as normal in captive Greys are not naturally exhibited in the wild. The stressful demands that domestic life imposes on our undomesticated birds often results in the suppression, displacement, or re-channeling of their natural behaviors into what we have come to regard as normal in our companion parrots.

Head Twitching

Head twitching is to be expected, for the most part, in Greys. If the ear canals are clear, clean, dry, and free of a feather shaft sticking into the ear, the twitching is probably normal. There are some disease processes and ingested toxins that cause tremors of the head but in the absence of these conditions, controlled twitching is normal.

Trembling Breast Feathers

The trembling movement of a resting Grey's breast feathers is normal. The resting heart rate of a 400 gram bird is 154 beats per minute; respiration at rest is 25-30 breaths per minute. The resting heart rate of a 500 gram bird is 147 beats per minute; respiration at rest is 20-30 breaths per minute. When the breast feathers are relaxed and slightly fluffed, these very light small feathers may tremble slightly in response to the heart beat and respiration.

Nail Biting

Nail biting or nail flicking is normal. Some Greys do it more than others do. It may be a grooming gesture although you will see it done more often by birds that are uncertain or anxious.

Digging

It is normal for Grey birds to do some digging. Although Greys can dig into adulthood, the frequency and duration of digging decreases significantly with age. However, Greys may dig for the following reasons that should be remedied:

Nail biting is a normal behavior.

- The perches may be too large or slippery.

- It's a release of energy.

- He wants more time out of his cage.

- He wants more human interaction.

- It's a habit he has developed.

If your bird's needs go unmet, the rate and intensity of digging can increase to a distressing level. The best approach to avoiding perseverative digging is to prevent the bird from developing a strong digging habit in the first place. First, carefully note the times your bird typically digs. Then, anticipate those times and provide an effective distraction such as putting the bird on top of his cage with a bowl of interesting food, moving him from his cage to his play area, cuddling him, or offering a new toy or treat from your hand.

Cage floor distractions often help reduce digging behavior. Place a small box or basket on the cage bottom filled with foot toys or other interesting items. Roll up a small magazine and wedge it in the cage bars at the bottom of the cage; twist and tie several lengths of paper towels to the cage bars near the bottom of the cage.

Posturing

Courting behavior, in even young birds, consists of bringing the "shoulders" (actually, the elbows) of their wings together in front of the chest. It is characterized by frequent twirling to display the white back and red tail, accompanied by soft grunting vocalizations. Courting behavior is normal.

Showing their red tails may be a species recognition signal. In other words, "I'm a Grey with a red tail. I'm not a Timneh with a maroon tail." Since Greys, the nominate species, and Timnehs, the sub species, can interbreed, it seems reasonable that a species recognition signal would exist. In breeding birds, the males twirl around frequently and display their back and tail to the female prior to mating.

Pumping

If the sides of the beak are stimulated by touch, even adult birds will "pump". Pumping is characterized by a rapid back and forth, bobbing motion. Some birds will hold onto a finger very tightly while pumping. This is normal.

In babies, pumping is a way of safely receiving regurgitated food quickly from the parents. A quick delivery would mean less noise from the peeping babies as they feed that might attract a predator and also frees the parent to forage for more food in a shorter period of time.

Regurgitation

Regurgitating is a normal and important natural instinct. It is a regular part of the behavior of the bonded pair; the male regurgitates to the hen so she can feed the babies; the hen regurgitates to the babies in the nestbox to feed them.

Even pre-weaned babies offer regurgitated food. Since the crop is a holding area, regurgitated food should be intact or at least recognizable. Vomiting arises from lower in the digestive tract and the difference in the appearance of the food is striking. Regurgitation is normal; vomiting is not.

Labored Breathing

Young unweaned babies don't have full use of their lungs and air sacs because the two grossly enlarged "stomachs" and the intestines take up the interior space of the body. Birds are thought of as flying machines and they are, except when they are babies: Baby birds are digestion machines. The whole body moves with inhalation and exhalation. What may appear to be labored breathing in an unweaned bird is an attempt to inflate the lungs and air sacs in a very crowded interior environment.

Persistent labored breathing, tail bobbing, or breathing with clicking, rasping or any other respiratory sounds in a bird of any age calls for an immediate visit to an avian vet.

The Rebellious Stage

At approximately six months and again at approximately eighteen months, it is normal for most Greys to enter a rebellious phase. They may test established rules and expectations just as a young human child would. For example, your bird may start climbing around the inside of the cage or hanging from the cage bars when asked to step up. He may refuse to step up from his perch or cage top, as well. He may suddenly start roaming or even biting in situations where no such behavior was previously seen.

Stay calm, gentle and resolute. Use your best facilitative teaching strategies to guide your bird to good behaviors and limit the opportunity for misbehavior (See the article, Living With Greys: Imposing Less, Facilitating More). This obstinacy or single-mindedness should be accepted for what it is—temporary.

Perhaps this rebelliousness has its roots in the natural behavior of Greys. Parents in the wild may begin to withdraw at around six months to encourage their babies' necessary independence. Although the youngster may still want the time and attention of the parents he may be compelled to push them away at the same time. The parents may know this is an important stage of development for their youngster and may encourage his shift of time and attention to food gathering techniques, association with other juveniles, and to the activities that produce competent coordination.

Do not worry that your sweet bird may be lost forever to irksome delinquency. Your bird may be attempting to become the independent juvenile required to become a successful adult. As our birds are clipped and caged for their safety, many of the natural behaviors are stifled by captivity. The rebellious actions we see may be a class of substitute behaviors for what would be occurring in nature.

Allowing Your Baby to Fully Fledge

Baby Greys who learn to fly with proficiency, control, and precision and who receive a custom wing trim don't injure themselves jumping or fluttering to the floor. Custom clipping a Grey means clipping the flight feathers depending on the strength and determination of the individual. Fully fledging means:

• The ability to bank in mid-air for course correction.

• The ability to hover in mid-air.

• The ability to land exactly where they intend to land consistently, with purpose and control.

After flight precision is achieved, the first four feathers should be clipped. The baby will make up for reduced power and lift by becoming stronger. This may take another couple of weeks. After the bird can again fly with precision and control, one feather at a time on each wing is clipped until a fifteen-foot glide path with no altitude gain is seen. Exhilaration with flight and headstrong determination enables a fledgling to fly farther with more flights clipped than will be possible at a later time in life.

Although it can be painful, figuratively and literally, watching a youngster learn to fly, there are ways to make your home relatively safe. While the bird is learning to fly, he will have crash and burn landings. This can't be avoided but his area should be made as safe as possible. Extreme caution is always necessary when a bird is learning to fly. Slightly close any blinds and close curtains or sheers so the impact is softer if the babies fly into the window. Restrict access to unsafe parts of the house. Close doors or hang a shower curtain on an expansion bar across the doorway to the rest of the house. All bathroom doors should be closed and toilet seats down. Never open a door to the outside unless you can see every bird that is out of the cage. Open outside doors with your back to them and the bird in your line of sight.

Mirrors can be plastered with temporary decals or bits of paper taped to them. Birds don't understand about glass and mirrors. Don't have standing water around—in the kitchen sink, mop pails, bathtubs of water, toilet bowls, etc. Don't cook with a flying baby or bird out of the cage. One bird I know was badly scalded when he landed in a colander of hot noodles draining in the kitchen sink. If expecting visitors, put the flying baby in his cage.

Keep a kitchen step stool handy for retrieving your bird from the chandeliers, atop drapery headers, window ledges, and other high places. Be very careful about other companion animals in a house with a bird that is learning to fly, and at other times too, of course. Never leave the bird alone in the room when he is out of his cage or leave him alone in the room with other companion animals. You can't teach a bird to fly; he has to learn on his own how to fly.

Abberrant Behaviors

Some commonly seen behaviors in pet birds are neither natural in the wild nor normal in your home. You must be informed and alert to the signs of a distressed Grey bird and succeed in providing solutions to his problems. It is not acceptable to give up on a bird, dismally passing it from home to home. And, it is most often totally unwarranted as solutions do exist for the patient and determined owner. Many of the aberrant behaviors that result in such inhumane treatment are the direct result of cruel or ignorant feeding and weaning strategies as indicated below.

Begging and Calling

A young Grey who has experienced hunger from underfeeding or forced weaning may beg out of habit. Begging and calling expend a great deal of energy more appropriately used for the exploration of the soft foods that should be provided. His begging behavior endures because the young bird believes, for a very long time, that he will be fed. Calling and begging are most unusual in well-fed and properly weaned Greys.

Pet owners who buy unweaned birds are often told the bird will eat when he is hungry enough. They may be told to ignore the crying, cover up the cage to stop the crying, not to handle, feed or take him from the cage until he stops crying. This advice is tragically, devastatingly wrong.

The anxiety associated with hunger that is ignored or punished is difficult to overcome as it damages the development of trust and security in your bird. You can not develop a loving relationship with a bird that is insecure and unable to trust his human caretakers. Isolating the bird teach him that humans ignore his most basic of needs for food and comfort. He learns that these cravings cause sensory deprivation and loneliness. This treatment cannot produce a tame, trusting, or well-behaved bird.

Begging, calling, and frantic climbing around in the cage is a message that should be heeded. Your bird is trying to communicate his need for food or companionship and comfort. Young post or pre-weaned birds like to be out of the cage for extended periods of time even when they haven't been unduly confined. Frequent periods of attention or play teach the bird that he will have companionship and attention again and again and again. He will soon realize that once he is locked in the cage, it won't be for hours and hours on end.

Promptly offering hot wet foods will be reassuring and satisfying. Offer a small feeding of formula or a hot wet food at the time a bird usually begs, in the morning or in the evening. This will help control his expression of food-related trauma. Lessening of the begging may not occur until the food leaves the crop and enters the digestive system. Only hunger and the anxiety associated with hunger will cause begging and calling. A properly fed weaning Grey does not cry for food. A begging, crying Grey is a sign that the bird is being starved in an effort to wean him or that he is not being fed enough during the pre-weaned period.

Other aberrant behaviors also surface when a Grey is weaned inappropriately or too early, whether this is done by a breeder, pet store clerk or pet owner. You may see the following problem behaviors in young birds that are weaned using deprivation or forced weaning methods:

- Phobic birds who are afraid of everything—including the caregiver.

- Youngsters fixated on the one food they have found that satisfies their hunger and they are unwilling to try new foods.

- Fearful uncertain birds without a sense of belonging or security.

- Feather mutilation or plucking in young birds.

- Anorexia.

- A weakened immune system.

- Small thin birds.

Re-fledging a Fearful Grey

An anxious, insecure, uncoordinated, clumsy, or fearful Grey who was never permitted to fledge can be re-fledged. It can take two or three years to bring such a bird to the place where he should have been at three or four months of age. The most advantageous time for a bird to learn to fly is the time determined by instinct and nature. It can be done later although with more difficulty.

As the flights grow out, clip the first couple. These are all alone with no "buddy" flights and are much more vulnerable to injury. The portion of the unfurling flight feather where the shaft is HARD is safe to clip. The living portion of the shaft is swollen, soft and you can see black, brown or red under the keratin sheath. Clip only the portion where the shaft is hard and mature at the end of the emerging flight.

As the other flights grow, clip each succeeding flight a little longer until they have "buddy" flights. Once the flights have support from adjacent flights, they are safer from injury. The bird will look a little ragged but the aim is to protect the first two or three or four flight feathers as they are most vulnerable. However, all emerging flights are at risk with a bird that has never learned to fly or land safely or has no control over his body.

This control is acquired from his previous flying experience. It may take a year or longer to coordinate the lengths of the flight feathers but the bird will still have enough power and lift to begin to practice flying. It's the first couple of flight feathers on each wing that needs the initial protection. Birds who know how to fly are much less likely to damage a blood feather when they begin to molt. It is preferable to let them learn to fly in the beginning than to re-fledge them. Extraordinary precautions against escape are required. Bird-proofing the house for the bird's safety is essential. Other companion animals have to be very carefully supervised and the bird that being re-fledged can never be left uncaged in the same room with them.

In Good Health

Prey animals are notorious for hiding ill health from the rest of their flock and predators. Determining and maintaining the health of your bird requires a comprehensive knowledge of many factors.

Weight Variations

African Greys vary widely in weight. This is normal. Weigh your bird daily from weaning until one year of age. Weigh him weekly after the age of one year. Record the daily or weekly weights. A bird that is losing weight should be seen immediately by an avian vet. Weight loss is serious business. The following factors may explain weight variation in pet birds.

First, the parents' African origin will have a profound influence on the weight of their babies. Greys from some countries or regions are larger than Greys from other regions. The sex of the bird also plays a role in weight. Generally, females are smaller and weigh less than males although there are large females and small males. The bird's age is another determining factor— adults are more muscular. An older bird of comparable conformation will weigh more than a juvenile.

Birds, like humans, improve their feeding skill over time. Although some male parents are naturally better providers than other males, experienced Grey parents are better feeders and thus have larger babies. Experienced human handfeeders typically do a better job of providing for Grey babies, as well.

Some babies just are better eaters than others. The "good" eaters gain more. If the baby bird slings, flings, or regurgitates formula, he will gain less well. Babies who are ill will not gain well. The quality, amount, and frequency of the food provided by the breeder to the parents can affect the weight of the babies. Grey babies in the wild are at the mercy of the available food. So too are our handraised babies but we can and must control this factor.

Underfeeding is common in domestic Greys who are sold unweaned. A young unweaned baby that is inadequately or infrequently fed will not grow to his full potential. The kind, amount, and frequency of formula fed by the handfeeder affects the weight of the babies. A handfed baby must have as much formula as he can digest and process on a regular basis. Skipped or late feedings must not occur.

Breast Muscles

According to Avian Medicine, "A normal adult bird should have solid, well formed, rounded pectoral muscles with a slight dip on either side of the sternum". The breast muscle should feel firm and meaty; the sternum or breastbone will feel slightly sharp and bony as it is not covered by the breast muscles. If the bird, when viewed at a slight angle, has slight cleavage, he isn't too thin.

Human Bacteria

Never feed your bird anything that has been in your mouth. The natural bacteria that are resident in humans can cause infections and disease in birds. If you have a cold or the flu, wash your hands before handling your bird. The bird has little to fear from human viruses, as most viruses are species specific, but the associated bacteria can be harmful. Influenza A may be one of the few human viruses that can infect birds.

Practice good hygiene and don't "give" anything to your bird. Kiss your bird on the upper curve of the beak. Avoid touching your bird's nostrils.

Buying Birds At a Bird Fair

Until we have all of necessary life-protecting vaccines for birds, such as are available for other companion animals, we have to be vigilant and guard our birds from exposure. Since it is much too difficult to determine the health status of a bird on sight, birds shouldn't be exposed to the birds of others. Many of the diseases of concern exhibit few or no symptoms in the early stages. Some, like PDD, exhibit symptoms or cause death years after exposure.

The leading killer of baby birds is polyomavirus. A baby is usually 35 days old when the first of two shots of vaccine is administered. The present Pacheco's vaccine is not routinely recommended. For other diseases of concern, such as PBFD, psittacosis, and PDD, there is no vaccine for them at present although avian research is ongoing. A baby is at the mercy of the sickest baby at the fair. A baby with an immature immune system shouldn't be in a place where he can be exposed to any disease.

Babies who are unsold at a bird fair should be permanently quarantined to protect the lives and health of the rest of the babies in such a breeder's facility. Whether you buy from a breeder to takes babies to a fair is something you have to determine based on your best judgement and the available research on the diseases of birds.

Pet stores And Window Shopping

Do not "window shop" in stores that have birds. Don't touch a bird in a pet store. A bird may be very ill and still appear healthy; never assume that a strange bird is healthy. Some of the really deadly viruses are stable in the environment. Don't handle other people's bird unless you are sure they have the same high standards you have. If you can't resist—leave your shoes in the garage, wash the clothes you were wearing, shower, wash your hair and change clothes before handling your own birds.

Don't buy anything for your birds, or yourself, from an open bin. Rodents are the prime vector for salmonella which is very dangerous to birds. Insects and circulated dust or grime may have contaminated the bin's contents. Buy from closed containers or buy food in the original sealed packaging.

Don't buy anything from a store that maintains its birds or other animals in poor conditions or that sells unweaned baby birds. Selling unweaned babies makes good economic sense. The sellers don't have to keep a Grey for months and months until he is weaned. Time is money. They can transfer the health problems, and the death risks, to the buyer.

Support places of business that maintain their animals humanely and provide a clean environment, clean cages, clean water, and clean healthy food.

Vote with your dollars.

Feather Patterns

Many new bird owners notice interesting feather patterns regarding coloration and replacement. In the case of the Grey, feathers do make the bird. (See the Grooming Your Bird section below for additional feather information.)

Tail Feathers

The color differences in the tail feathers of the redtail Grey and Timneh Grey are striking—for the immatures and for the adults. Immature Greys will have dark margins on the tail feathers. This is normal. By the end of the two-year molt cycle, your bird should have his adult plumage and his bright red tail.

The color of the tail feathers in baby Timnehs is quite variable. It can range from dark maroon to light maroon and from a very dark gray to light gray. The uppertail coverts in baby Timnehs are a bright red. This color usually molts out. The uppertail coverts in adult Timnehs are grey with some maroon occasionally. The tail coverts are the short overlapping feathers that cover the base of the tail feathers—both on the underside and the upper side of the tail.

Red Feathers

Red feathering is common in handfed Greys and Timnehs. Usually red feathers will molt out although some Greys will have red feathers into adulthood. The red feathers of youngsters are usually seen under the wings, on the flanks, and on the legs.

Visible Sex Differences Between Greys

Generally, immature females will have a gray edging to the undertail coverts. The males usually will not have this gray edging. The undertail coverts form a "v" and lay against the long tail feathers. Adult Grey females almost invariably have undertail coverts with grey edging.

Molting

A Grey's first molt begins at around 8 months of age. Diet, health status, the amount and quality of light affect the duration and frequency of the molt. Companion birds that are indoors may molt feathers a little at a time all year long. Some will have a heavy or moderate molt once a year, others will have a lighter molt a couple of times a year.

Large psittacine birds have a two-year molt cycle. In other words, it will take about two years for every feather on the body to be replaced by new feathers. A bird will have feathers of different ages on the body at the same time. The third molt, within the two-year period, should result in mature plumage in a normal bird. The first molt is considered to be the replacement of the neonatal down with feathers.

According to <u>Avian Medicine</u>, the progression of the molt is head, neck, body, then the wing and tail feathers. To reiterate, the replacement of all of the feathers on the body will take about two years.

A feather that is ready to molt is loose in the shaft and will appear to fall out when a bird shakes or ruffles his feathers to settle them into place. It is normal for down feathers to be shed continually. Birds whose bodies don't have the required reserves may delay molting. Malnourished birds, ill birds, or those who are exposed to inadequate light may have an incomplete molt, a delayed molt, or a shorter than normal duration molt.

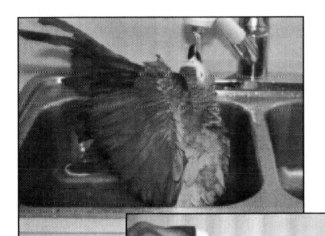

Whether your bird enjoys a full bath in the sink or misting, routine bathing is a must.

Molting is done by degrees and in an orderly fashion. Feather tracts are molted in a progressive fashion. A bird should never have bare patches. He shouldn't molt all of the tail feathers or flight feathers at any one time. These vitally important feathers, required for flight and safety from predators in the wild, are molted in an orderly fashion. Progressive molting of the feathers ensures that birds can still fly. In captivity, molting isn't the life and death matter that it is in the wild.

Birds who are molting should be bathed on a daily basis. Molting can make the bird feel unbearably itchy and it is painful to have new pins working their way through the skin. Adequate skin and feather hydration may prevent plucking or feather mutilation during molting, and other times as well. Molting birds also require extra nourishment, especially protein, during the molt as their metabolism speeds up and their appetite increases, sometimes dramatically.

Grooming Your Bird

Routine grooming by a bird's trusted owner is often less stressful than grooming by a stranger. With some initial guidance and care, you can learn to groom your own bird.

Baths

Keeping one's feathers hydrated and clean is a natural behavior for Grey birds. Don't underestimate your birds' need for bathing especially in the drier months of the year or when you are heating your home. Don't give up. It is a matter of discovering which method your bird prefers or at the least, will tolerate.

In captivity, you must arrange the opportunity for your

bird to bath daily. If it is started very early, when they are partially feathered, Greys learn that a bath is just a fact of life. Some like it, some love it, some hate it, some tolerate it, some huddle in misery waiting for it to end. Experiment to discover the bathing method that your bird likes or will tolerate.

Your bird might prefer a shower. If he is perching securely, he can be taken to the bathroom and allowed to observe your shower from a distance; for example, on the shower curtain rod out of the force of the water. Place a damp towel or washcloth on the shower perch or wrap it with Vet Wrap to provide a more secure footing. Ensure that your bird does not fall as this scare may generalize fear to this method of bathing.

A special shower perch will give your bird some degree of autonomy as he will be able to move in or out of water spray. Don't move faster with bathing than he is willing to follow; allow him to become accustomed to the sound and look of the falling water. The temperature of the bath water is an important concern to some Greys. Some will only enjoy bathing in cool water, others prefer warm. Experiment to see which your bird prefers.

Another approach to bathing is to place your bird on the rim of the tub on a damp towel or washcloth for foot security, while you laugh and play in the water. If the water is shallow, he can be placed in it after he watches you for a while. A floating child's toy may be of interest to him. Some birds will bathe in the kitchen sink. Run a shallow pool of water in the sink. Place a cloth on the bottom of the sink for footing. Gently place your bird in the sink with or without the water lightly running.

Other birds prefer bathing in a very large dog crock or large flower pot holder. Some owners put salad leaves or toys in the wa-

ter to intrigue the bird. Spray bathing is commonly accepted by Greys. It can be done with the specialty sprays that produce a fine mist or fog or with the old-fashioned spray bottle. Spray your bird so that the water drops gently onto his body.

Effective Restraint for Grooming

It is normal for even the most loving Grey to need gentle restraining when having his toenails and flight feathers groomed. Clippers and scissors can be dangerous around an unrestrained bird. The first step in grooming your bird is to learn how to restrain him safely, gently and effectively with the following method:

Double fold a bath towel; protect your hands in the folds on the outside of the towel; capture the bird from the side; position the wings against his body comfortably. Position a longer portion of the towel over the bird's head than you might think necessary. This will protect your fingers and hands. Be careful not to compress the chest—birds have no diaphragm and breathe by expanding the chest. Avoid touching the bird's eyes with the towel. Grasp the bird under the jaws with the thumb and long finger. Keep the neck straight. It is difficult to strangle a bird but there is no need to grasp him tightly. A bird's esophagus and trachea are surrounded by bone. This is unlike humans whose esophagus and trachea are partially surrounded by a "c" shaped bone structure.

Toenail Clipping

It is normal for a pet bird to need your help keeping his toenails groomed. If the bird has appropriately sized perches and access to a cement perch, he will require less frequent toenail clipping. Due to the length of a Grey's toes, a larger diameter cement perch is best—the size intended for cockatoos works well.

The cat's-claw or bird's-claw type clippers produce the cleanest cut. The cutting edge of this clipper cuts around the circumference of the toenail. The dog clippers will squeeze the nail as they cut and create a ragged edge.

By clipping a little off the end of the nail once a month or so, the vein will eventually recede as it does with cats and dogs. When the vein recedes, there will be less chance of the nail bleeding. African Greys need to have their nails a little longer than some other species for perching stability and security.

If there is bleeding from the clipped toenail, the safest blood stopper is a paste of Aloe Vera Gel and cornstarch. Aloe has soothing properties and is preferable for most pain management. There are no chemicals or toxic substances in cornstarch. Keep the opened bottle of Aloe in the 'fridge and mix up a small amount of the paste when needed.

You can pack and tap Quik Stop into the end of the bleeding nail and hold the toe with gentle pressure on the sides of the toe. The veins that feed the toe are located here. This should stop the bleeding. Quik Stop should never be used on flesh or on a bleeding blood feather.

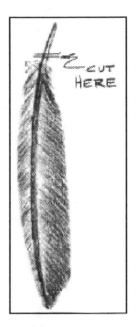

Silver nitrate sticks can be used to stop toenail bleeding. However, silver nitrate causes death of tissue and should NEVER be used on flesh. The sticks should wrapped in paper or foil and stored in a cool dark place.

Trimming Flight Feathers of Fledged Greys

The specifics of trimming flight feathers are discussed in-depth in another article in this book and have been discussed above. It is mentioned here in the context of routine grooming of your post-fledged bird. Once a fledgling has reaped the physical and emotional benefits of learning to fly, it is essential that your bird become accustomed to a non-flying lifestyle to prevent him experiencing the tragic accidents that will invariably befall him in your home.

It is true that flying for birds is natural and allowing your fledgling to learn to fly has great benefits for your bird's coordinated movements and confidence; however, flying by windows, open doors, and boiling spaghetti pots is not natural; it is, simply, indefensibly reckless. Keeping our grown birds restricted from flight is one of the many compensations we must make to keep our pet birds safe.

Greys differ in strength and determination. Recently weaned babies who have fledged are very strong from exercise. A clip that prevents a gain in altitude in a recently weaned bird is not suitable for an older bird. Older birds that have been clipped as youngsters need fewer flights clipped after they molt. As a rule, a fledg-

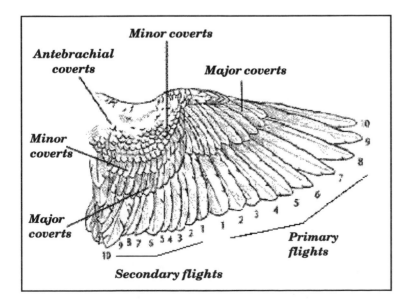

Antebrachial coverts
Minor coverts
Major coverts
Minor coverts
Major coverts
Primary flights
Secondary flights

Major c

ling may need as many as six or seven flights clipped; an older bird that has not had exercise flying will do nicely with four flights clipped. If the older bird can flutter or fly more than 15 feet, clip an additional flight feather from feather each wing—irrespective of altitude considerations. Altitude is, however, the most important thing to avoid.

A bird should not be taken out-of-doors unless he is in a cage or carrier—whether wing-clipped or not. Even a flightless bird out-of-doors uncaged or unconfined can flutter into the mouth of a dog or cat or into the path of a bicycle or car.

Emerging Blood Feathers

As the first new flights emerge, they are vulnerable to injury or a break from a clumsy landing because they don't have the physical support of adjacent flight feathers to protect them. The unfurling portion of the feather below the living part of the feather shaft can be clipped safely as it unfurls. Never under any circumstances clip into the swollen, soft, blood-filled, living portion of the shaft—clip only the unfurled feather at the end of the shaft. The mature feather shaft, farthest from the body, is clear, hollow, and quite hard. Once the supporting feathers emerge, the early ones don't need to be clipped any more. The bird's wing flight feathers will be uneven after being clipped as the new flights unfurl but there will be less chance of a broken blood feather or other injury.

Beak Trimming

It is seldom necessary to groom, trim, or shorten a Grey's beak. If a Grey, or any companion bird, requires repeated beak trimming or exhibits uneven wear of the beak, he should receive a diagnostic evaluation from an avian vet to determine the reason. Some nutritional deficiencies and/or disease processes can cause the beak to

overgrow and an avian vet should assess such a bird.

Providing a healthy bird with wooden toys for chewing, a bark covered branch or cement perch to groom his beak on, ample climbing or clambering opportunities for beak exercise should be sufficient to keep the beak in good condition. To determine if the beak needs to be groomed follow the guidelines below:

Look at the bird in profile. If the TIP of the upper mandible is BELOW an imaginary horizontal line drawn straight outward starting from bottom of the LOWER mandible (closest to the body), the beak needs to be trimmed or groomed. If the tip is above this line, then the beak doesn't need to be groomed.

Diet Concerns

Diet is an area of great concern for all pet bird owners. A bird cannot be emotionally or physically healthy, at any stage in his life, without a varied and abundant diet.

Humane Weaning of the Older Baby

Sometimes a baby will refuse to give up eating formula because the wrong types of foods are being offered to facilitate weaning. If your bird is "overdue" on his weaning schedule, don't offer large quantities of low calorie fresh fruits or vegetables. Doing so may be the reason why the overdue baby is reluctant to give up the formula. Calorie-dense formula satisfies his hunger; fresh fruits and many veggies do not. Why should he give up the one food that satisfies his hunger?

Offer instead high calorie foods like baked sweet potato, baked winter squash, boiled popcorn kernels, a beans/grains mix and, most importantly, "birdie bread". Very small pieces of fresh fruits and veggies can be offered but only for color and variety. Pellets should be available at all times. Offering a variety of pellets may ensure he will find one that he prefers. Prepare and offer several bowls of the soft foods daily. Once the baby is eating these more nutritious foods, the breeder formulation pellet and the calorie-dense soft foods, the amount of formula at the morning meal can be reduced by 5 cc each day over 10 days or so. When he is off the morning feeding, start on the evening feeding in the same way.

If you are offering a maintenance pellet, it may not be providing enough nourishment for a weaning or young bird. Offer a hi-potency or breeder formulation pellet until a Grey is one year of age. Weigh him daily after the morning bomb and before breakfast. Record the daily weight. If he loses more than five grams, add back the amount of formula you reduced the day before and continue with the gradual reduction the next day. Don't hesitate to add back a reduction in the formula amount. Don't let him go hungry. Keep a careful eye on his consumption of the weaning foods. A hungry baby will be very reluctant to wean.

An excellent transition food is soaked warmed primate biscuits. These biscuits are a warm soft food that is psychologically satisfying. Offering biscuits to a weaning bird several times a day will satisfy his hunger during the time when the amount of formula is gradually reduced.

I recommend only Zupreem brand primate biscuits in the original packaging. Store the biscuits in the freezer until you are ready to use them. Soak in very hot water (not boiling—they will dissolve) until they are soft, for about 15 minutes. Cover the small bowl you are soaking them in with a lid or small plate to speed the softening and retain the warmth. Gently squish the biscuit against a pad of paper towels to remove excess wa-

ter. Cut each biscuit into small pieces. If the pieces need to be warmed, they can be zapped in the microwave for 7 or 8 seconds. Test each piece by gently squeezing it to be sure it doesn't have any hot spots. If it is too hot, it will burn the crop just like overheated formula.

You should be able to wean him in two or three or four weeks using this method. True weaning will depend on how well he accepts the foods I suggest you offer.

Spray Millet

The tiny, dry, lightweight hulls from spray millet can easily be inhaled. Many reports exist of birds inhaling millet hulls into the nostrils, the sinuses, and the lungs or getting a hull caught in their throats. Very young birds just learning to eat weaning foods are especially at risk for inhaling hulls. Young birds have to learn to coordinate swallowing and breathing.

Placing the spray of millet in a large bowl of water and microwaving it for 15 minutes may avoid the light flyaway hulls and reduce the risk of inhalation and injury.

Peanuts

Peanuts are a notorious source of aflatoxin. If aflatoxin is inhaled a bird may develop Aspergillosis. Aspergillus is ubiquitous in the environment. Humans and birds have a natural immunity to it or they would be overwhelmed by infection with such constant exposure. However, when a bird's immune system is compromised as with a secondary bacterial infection or stress, and aflatoxin is inhaled, a bird is at risk for aspergillosis. Aflatoxin can enter the body through surface to skin contact as well as through inhalation.

Mycotoxins, the by-product of molds, can cause liver toxicity if ingested. Mycotoxins are stable in the presence of heat and typical processing for human consumption. Control of these toxic compounds is accomplished by good harvesting techniques and by storing peanuts properly.

The degree of physical damage to a bird can vary according to the type of toxin and the bird's nutritional and health status.

Reconsider feeding your bird peanuts. There is nothing nutritionally to be gained from peanuts that can not be similarly gained from safer foods.

Vitamins in Your Birds Water

Don't put vitamins in your bird's water. Bacteria can explode in this nutrient rich medium and the vitamins lose potency rapidly. If the water tastes "off", the birds will be reluctant to drink it, which is a serious problem as well. A constant source of clean fresh tasty water is essential for good health. Birds that are on a pellet-based diet don't require additional vitamins. The potential for over-dosing and toxicity is a real concern if unneeded and unnecessary supplements are offered to your birds.

Iron

Plants, such as nuts, beans and grains, contain iron that is safe for Greys. If iron is added to a product, the federal government requires that that it be listed on the label. Watch the product labels for added iron supplements. According to Avian Medicine, iron is poorly absorbed from the gastrointestinal tract. Moderate excessive consumption of iron in the diet of a healthy Grey bird should not cause toxicity, however, more iron is available to your bird from animal sources than from vegetable sources. Less than 5% of the iron from plant sources is assimilated; from animal sources, the figure is approximately 20-25%.

The Cage and Home Environment

There are many considerations to providing a safe and stimulating environment for your bird. The conditions of your home as well as his home within your home, his cage, need ongoing attention. The choice of an appropriate cage, perches that provide secure footing, food bowls with bird-safe holders, coupled with regular cleaning will give you assurance that your bird will have a safe, healthy place to live.

Air Borne Toxins

A lot of oxygen is required for flight and birds process air very efficiently. When humans breathe, the air is contained within our lungs. When birds breathe, the air is circulated throughout the body via the lungs and air sacs. A bird's lungs and air sacs are much more efficient than humans who have small lungs relative to their size.

Air borne toxins are distributed throughout your birds body with deadly efficiency. Inhaled toxic vapors, cigarette smoke, radon gas, toxic by-products of chemicals, heated non-stick coatings, smoke from fires, odors or fumes from self-cleaning ovens, scented candles, room or auto air "fresheners", particles from carpet fresheners, aerosol propellants, and heated or burning resins or coatings on new ovens or ceramic stovetops, to name a few, can be deadly to birds as these substances are too quickly circulated throughout the body.

As radon is a powerful carcinogen, all homes should be tested for radon gas emission—for the birds and for the humans. The other substances listed above should not be used anywhere near your birds. Consider the extent to which these toxins will be circulated through your home via heating and air-cooling vents and avoid them diligently.

The Cage

A bird's size and activity level are important considerations when purchasing a cage. A suitable cage size for a Grey is at least three feet wide and two feet deep. Height

isn't very important, as there are few dominance issues with Greys.

A playpen top with a tray is desirable. The tray will catch the droppings and keep them from falling on the perches or in the food cups inside the cage. "Out" time is very important for your bird, and if the playpen has toys and food cups attached, he can have a snack or play safely. Some birds prefer to sit on the open cage door in spite of having a playpen top. A newspaper spread under the cage door can protect your carpet. A cement perch can be attached to the outside of the cage bars above the door as a change of location for sitting, napping or just contemplating the world.

Don't house your bird in a round cage. Converging bars can trap toes or feet. Square cages offer more interior room and provide a place for a pie shaped corner perch.

Leave the bottom grate in the cage so your bird doesn't have access to the waste tray. The droppings and the food in the bottom of the cage provide a good growing environment for bacteria, fungi, and mold spores. Change the papers frequently.

Organic bedding, such as crushed nut shells, grass pellets, ground corncobs, and kitty litter type products can cause illness and death if ingested. The dust associated with these products can be harmful. Newspaper is free and safe. Toxic inks haven't been used for newspaper printing since the 1970s. The colored portions of the newspaper and the slick colored sections are also non-toxic.

Wipe down the cage bars daily using detergent and water or a bird safe disinfectant solution. It's not necessary to maintain your bird's cage in a hospital-sanitary manner, but clean surroundings are obviously more conducive to good health. If you have other birds, wash your hands between cages when cleaning or changing papers.

Covering the Cage

An important consideration in whether or not to cover the cage is the possibility that the bird will chew on the cloth covering and ingest the fabric. Serious blockage of the digestive system—and possibly death—can occur from the ingestion of any fabric. Any fraying of the cover should be trimmed away daily to prevent entanglement.

An additional consideration is that the covered bird is in a closed environment with the powder down dust, pieces of pellets, and the droppings in the waste tray.

A covered bird can be startled in the night and awake in a pitch-dark cage. Falling from the perch or thrashing in the cage can cause injury or provoke a phobic or panic episode. A nightlight and an uncovered cage can prevent these episodes.

If the house is drafty or the bird is in front of a window, covering a portion of the cage would provide nighttime comfort. If the windows are air tight, moving the cage out about three feet from the window would avoid subjecting the bird to cold air radiating from the windowpanes.

Food Bowls

Many cages come with too few bowls. There should be a bowl for pellets, soft foods, water, and a treat bowl. Some birds are "dumpers" and will need to have lock-down cups or heavy crock dishes. Use ten ounce bowls for water, pellets, and treats. Greys don't drink a lot of water so a large bowl is unnecessary. A small bowl is large enough for a day's supply of pellets. A large diameter 20 ounce bowl for soft foods allows the bird to look his food over. If he can see and get at his favorite foods, he is less likely to toss food looking for his favorites. Crumble up the "birdie bread" and mix it with the beans/grains mixture and the sprouts. Cut up the fresh fruits and vegetables into small pieces; if only one bite is taken, only a small piece of food will be dropped or flung.

Lock-down stainless steel bowls with acrylic holders will prevent your bird from dumping his food and water. The bowls are indestructible; the holders are safe and don't take up interior room.

If crocks are used, the crock holders should have a bowl in them to prevent the bird from becoming trapped inside the ring and possibly injured. The bowl can be filled with small foot toys. Deaths have occurred when birds have gotten themselves trapped in these rings.

All cups must be scrubbed with a brush every day using hot water and detergent or

Lockdown cups prevent your bird from dumpting his food or water. Stainless steel makes cleaning quick and easy.

run through the dishwasher. Avoid simply re-filling the pellet cup. Put clean food into clean dishes. Position the cups so that the bird can't poop in them. Some birds will perch on the edges of the cups and you may find you will have to wash the cup and change the water during the day. Separate the pellet and water cups to avoid "dunking". Bacteria like pellets, too.

Perches

The perches in most cages are placed at a level determined by the manufacturer. If a change of location is desired and the perch is slotted, it may have to be replaced by a bird safe wood branch. A hole can be drilled in each end of the replacement perch and it can be attached to the cage bars with heavy plastic or stainless steel fender washers inside and out. The perches must be positioned low enough so that the bird has sufficient headroom. A bird should be able to completely spread his wings, sit comfortably on the perch and not have any part of his body touch the cage bars.

Natural branches are the best and least expensive perch. The variation in diameter and the surface irregularities make branches the most comfortable and the healthiest perching surface. Birds can develop foot problems and pressure points on the bottom of the feet if given only smooth perches such as wooden or plastic dowels.

The natural branch, with the bark left on, should come from a tree that has not been sprayed with pesticides. The branch can be scrubbed several times with a brush, hot water and detergent to remove surface dirt, loose bark, moss, and algae. After rinsing thoroughly, it can be disinfected with a bird-safe disinfectant. The branch can also be scrubbed as above and baked in a 350F degree oven for 20 minutes to sterilize it.

Refer to the recommended reading URLs for a more complete listing of bird-safe wood. Use only fresh green branches—not fallen or dead. Don't use branches from trees whose fruit contains a stone, such as peach and cherry. Some safe woods include citrus, ash, magnolia, willow, apple, crabapple, elm, dogwood, madrona, guava, birch, and sassafras.

The perches, depending on the size of the bird's foot, should vary along the length from one and one-half inches to approximately two and one-half inches.

A large diameter perch is generally more comfortable than small diameter perch. The feet and toes don't get cramped on a large perch like they do with a perch whose diameter is too small. The usual recommendation is that the toes should go two-thirds of the way around the perch, however, I believe this diameter perch is too small. The toenails should touch the surface of the perch. Offer a variety of sizes, textures and perching surfaces.

For a young bird, unaltered manzanita is too slippery. Injuries can occur from slipping or falling, especially in the dark. If a

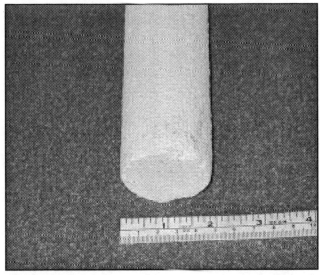

Whether you use a natural perch or a cement perch the proper diameter is extremely important for your bird's feet and comfort.

bird is unable to perch without slipping or falling, his confidence can be affected.

Position the perches so that the bird can stand comfortably and eat or drink from his cups. Since most birds hold their food in their feet, the perches can accumulate food particles and should be washed down frequently.

Medical Services

Yearly health exams and other medical services are essential to the proper care and well-being of your precious Grey. An experienced avian veterinarian is essential as well. Never hesitate to ask questions and question authority. This devoted attitude is most often understood and appreciated by your vet and your bird's life may depend on it.

Health Exams

Birds are masters at hiding the symptoms of illness. It pays big dividends for a prey animal like a bird to **appear** to be healthy. If you look "normal" and act "normal", the predator will not target you. Predators prefer an easy meal and a sick bird is an easy meal. Our birds are still wild animals and still hide the symptoms of illness. By the time a bird looks sick or acts sick, he is **very** sick indeed.

Annual health exams are one of the best ways to make **sure** our birds live long healthy lives. Minor or insignificant changes are meaningful and when they occur, the bird should be taken to the vet.

If your vet refuses to perform blood tests, find another vet. No vet can look at a bird and tell if the bird is anemic or has low blood calcium or is suffering from some viral, bacterial or fungal infection. Only tests, screens, and cultures can do this. The exam should include:

1. Complete Blood Count.

2. Gram's Stain. Some vets routinely do a Culture and Sensitivity in addition to or instead of a Gram's Stain. Both the Gram's Stain and/or the Culture and Sensitivity should be comprised of a two-site sampling—the feces and the mouth/throat.

3. Blood Calcium Level test.

4. Thorough and complete physical examination.

Since the symptoms of an abnormally low blood calcium level are so devastating in Greys, including tremors, seizures, convulsions, and irregular heartbeat, every African Grey should have a blood calcium level screen run at least once a year. This is a part of the Blood Chemistry Panel and not a part of the Complete Blood Count.

A PBFD (Psitttacine Beak and Feather Disease) screen should be done at the initial exam, particularly if the breeder or pet store provides a time-based health guarantee.

The polyomavirus vaccine booster can be administered at the annual exam. While polyoma is the leading killer of baby birds, some adults die too. A complete Blood Chemistry Panel can be a useful baseline to compare results against if there are suspected or actual health problems in the future. It is up to the owner to be as fully informed as possible and to be a partner in the fullest sense with the avian vet in the management of the health of his birds. No question should be too trivial for the vet to answer and to explain for as long as it takes until you understand.

The following articles and papers may be helpful to you in deciding what procedures to have performed on your bird:

• Complete Blood Count, Scott McDonald DVM

• The Nit pickers Physical Exam or Beyond Upright and Feathered Fern Van Sant DVM

• Chlamydia Psittaci (Parrot Fever) Infection in Companion Birds Dr. Thomas Tully, Jr. DVM

• Compendium of Psittacosis (Chlamydiosis) Control 1997 National Association of State Public Health Veterinarians Inc.

• Prevention of Avian Polyomavirus Infections through Vaccination (January 1996) Branson W. Ritchie, DVM, PHD, Kenneth S. Latimer, DVM, PHD, Cheryl B.Greenacre, DVM, Denise Pesti, MS, Raymond Campagnoli, MS, Phil D. Lukert, DVM, PhD

• PBFD Diagnostic Flowchart modified from the Proceedings of the International Aviculturists Society, January 13-16, 1994

Bands and Band Removal

It is normal for your pet bird to wear a band. However, occasionally reasons to remove the band do arise such as leg injuries, leg feather abrasion, or excessive nibbling in the band area. It is not necessary to anesthetize a bird to remove band, but GREAT care MUST be taken with band removal. If an inexperienced person tries to remove it, a broken leg can easily result. Bands are hard and hollow leg bones are fragile. Do not permit the band to be removed unless you are present and NEVER allow a layperson or inexperienced vet attempt it.

The proper equipment is vital to avoid a broken leg. Such equipment includes locking vise grips along with a heavy-duty metal cutter or a water-cooled Dremel with a metal grinding tip.

Keep the band and ask the vet to enter the band number in your bird's medical folder. Also, ask for a dated letter on your vet's letterhead stationary stating that the band was removed along with the number and other information on the band.

A closed band is placed on a domestic baby bird at a time when the foot is small enough to slide the band over it. It is a flat band with no opening. An open band is usually stainless steel and is put on the leg of imported birds. Open bands pose entanglement dangers and should be removed. The open band looks like a wedding ring with an opening in it.

Microchipping

Microchipping is a permanent type of identification. The chip, about the size of a grain of rice, is implanted in the breast muscle. It doesn't migrate as it is encased in protective strands of fiber produced by the bird's body. A small drop of surgical glue may be used on the injection site. There is no energy source in the chip; it is inert. It is read in a similar way that the scanners in the supermarket read bar codes.

Only a chip in a sterile sealed package with a one-time syringe should be used. So-called "bulk chips" that come in bulk in one package may be cheaper but are more dangerous because they require sterilization along with the syringe. Never permit a bulk chip to be inserted in your bird.

Only an avian vet should implant the chip. Such a vet is more likely to understand the anatomy of a bird and know the location of blood vessels in the area.

Airlines and Birds

The airlines require that the carrier fit under the seat in front of you. The approved carrier is about 8 inches high; the entire top opens up. There is a small wire or plastic door in the top portion of the carrier and vertical air slots in the bottom portion of the carrier. Since it can be cold on the floor of the plane, cut a portion of a large towel to fit over the carrier and cover the air slots in the bottom portion of the carrier. Cut a slit in it for the handle.

A low crock can be put in the carrier, filled with soft foods plus grapes, apples, or oranges. Water will spill. The juicy fruits will provide more than enough fluid for the bird. Some airlines permit one or two live animals in the passenger compartment per flight and advance reservations are usually required. Some airlines permit no live animals in the passenger compartment.

Some states require a health certificate for a live animal. Whether a health paper is required or not, by the state or by the airline, it is always safest to have one with you. If anyone asks to see it, you must be able to produce it. The usual requirement is that the health paper has to be dated 10 days prior to the flight. The airline agents will explain their regulations and requirements upon request.

NOTES:

Bird's Weight Records

You may duplicate this sheet and use for each of your birds.

Bird's Name	Bird's Name	Bird's Name
Hatch Date:	Hatch Date:	Hatch Date:
Month/Year	Month/Year	Month/Year
1	1	1
2	2	2
3	3	3
4	4	4
5	5	5
6	6	6
7	7	7
8	8	8
9	9	9
10	10	10
11	11	11
12	12	12
13	13	13
14	14	14
15	15	15
16	16	16
17	17	17
18	18	18
19	19	19
20	20	20
21	21	21
22	22	22
23	23	23
24	24	24
25	25	25
26	26	26
27	27	27
28	28	28
29	29	29
30	30	30
31	31	31

Bird's Weight Records   *You may duplicate this sheet and use for each of your birds.*

Bird's Name	
Hatch Date:	
	Month/Year
1	
2	
3	
4	
5	
6	
7	
8	
9	
10	
11	
12	
13	
14	
15	
16	
17	
18	
19	
20	
21	
22	
23	
24	
25	
26	
27	
28	
29	
30	
31	

Bird's Name	
Hatch Date:	
	Month/Year
1	
2	
3	
4	
5	
6	
7	
8	
9	
10	
11	
12	
13	
14	
15	
16	
17	
18	
19	
20	
21	
22	
23	
24	
25	
26	
27	
28	
29	
30	
31	

Bird's Name	
Hatch Date:	
	Month/Year
1	
2	
3	
4	
5	
6	
7	
8	
9	
10	
11	
12	
13	
14	
15	
16	
17	
18	
19	
20	
21	
22	
23	
24	
25	
26	
27	
28	
29	
30	
31	

Important Phone Numbers

Name:	Name:
Address	Address
City/Zip:	City/Zip:
Phone/email:	Phone/email:
Name:	Name:
Address	Address
City/Zip:	City/Zip:
Phone/email:	Phone/cmail:
Name:	Name:
Address	Address
City/Zip:	City/Zip:
Phone/email:	Phone/email:
Name:	Name:
Address	Address
City/Zip:	City/Zip:
Phone/email:	Phone/email:
Name:	Name:
Address	Address
City/Zip:	City/Zip:
Phone/email:	Phone/email:
Name:	Name:
Address	Address
City/Zip:	City/Zip:
Phone/email:	Phone/email:
Name:	Name:
Address	Address
City/Zip:	City/Zip:
Phone/cmail:	Phone/email:
Name:	Name:
Address	Address
City/Zip:	City/Zip:
Phone/email:	Phone/email:

Important Phone Numbers

Name:	Name:
Address	Address
City/Zip:	City/Zip:
Phone/email:	Phone/email:
Name:	Name:
Address	Address
City/Zip:	City/Zip:
Phone/email:	Phone/email:
Name:	Name:
Address	Address
City/Zip:	City/Zip:
Phone/email:	Phone/email:
Name:	Name:
Address	Address
City/Zip:	City/Zip:
Phone/email:	Phone/email:
Name:	Name:
Address	Address
City/Zip:	City/Zip:
Phone/email:	Phone/email:
Name:	Name:
Address	Address
City/Zip:	City/Zip:
Phone/email:	Phone/email:
Name:	Name:
Address	Address
City/Zip:	City/Zip:
Phone/email:	Phone/email:

Recommended Reading

Some of the following articles, publications, and web sites are referenced in this publication or are considered helpful.

"A - Z of Zinc Poisoning"
Carol Highfill, *Winged Wisdom*
www.birdsnways.com/wisdom/ww14eiii.htm

"African Grey Variations"
Jean Pattison, Grey Play Roundtable
www.africangreys.com/articles/other/variations.htm

Jean Pattison, The African Queen
members.tripod.com/The_African_Queen/

"Artificial Incubation Applied to Small Numbers of Altricial Bird Eggs"
Mark Hagen
shell.pubnix.net/~mhagen/docu/incub1.html

"Aspergillosis Part I"
Linda Pesek DVM, The Aviary
theaviary.com/s1295-60.shtml

"Aspergillosis Part II"
Linda Pesek DVM, The Aviary
theaviary.com/s1295-61.shtml

"Aspergillosis"
Diane Wanamaker, Certified Avian Specialist
www.realmacaw.com/pages/asper1.html

"Aspergillus Part 1"
Nancy E. Masters
www.iape.org/Features/AspergillusPart01/

"Aspergillus Part 2"
Nancy E. Masters
www.iape.org/Features/AspergillusPart02/index.htm

Avian Art
www.parrottalk.com/art.htm

"The Avian Patient: Handling, Restraint, Anesthesia and Nursing Care"
Angela M. Lennox, DVM

www.vet.purdue.edu/vettech/VM204/LABORATO-RY/Avian%20notes.doc

"Basic Avian Clinical Pathology Testing"
Heidi L. Hoefer, DVM, Dip ABVP-Avian Practice
www.heidihoefer.com/pages/birds/avian_blood_test.htm

"Baubles, Bangles and Beads…Toys FAQ"
Anne Johnson, *Winged Wisdom*
www.birdsnways.com/wisdom/ww5e.htm

C & L Aviaries
www.claviaryonline.com/

"Calcium, Phosphorus & Vitamin D3 in Your Bird's Diet"
Carol Highfill, *Winged Wisdom*
www.birdsnways.com/wisdom/ww22eii.htm

"Chlamydia Psittaci (Parrot Fever) Infections In Companion Birds"
Thomas Tully, Jr. DVM
www.parrottalk.com/chlamydia.html

"Citricidal: Cure & Disinfectant"
Carolyn Swicegood, *Winged Wisdom*
www.birdsnways.com/wisdom/ww26eiii.htm

"Common Parrot Behavioral Myths & Why They Are Myths"
Sally Blanchard
www.companionparrot.com/articles/myths.html

"Compendium of Psittacosis (Chlamydiosis) Control 1997"
National Assoc. of State Public Health Veterinarians
www.funnyfarmexotics.com/IAS/psittac.htm

"Complete Blood Count"
Scott McDonald DVM
www.parrottalk.com/cbc.html

"Cornell University Database of Material Safety Data Sheets"
msds.pdc.cornell.edu/msdssrch.asp
www.msdssearch.com/DBLinksN.htm

"Dangers of Soft PVC Toys & Vinyl Products"
Carol Highfill, *Winged Wisdom*
birdsnways.com/wisdom/ww18eiv.htm

Diplomates of the American Board of Veterinary Practitioners, Certified in Avian Practice
www.birdsnways.com/articles/abvpvets.htm

"Disease Prevention Through Proper Sanitation and Disinfection in an Indoor Psittacine Breeding Facility"
Mark Hagen
shell.pubnix.net/~mhagen/docu/disease1.html#Disease

"Feather Disorders in Pet Birds"
Mark Hagen
pubnix.net/~mhagen/docu/b_disord.html

"Feather Mutilation"
Anne Johnson, *Winged Wisdom*
www.birdsnways.com/wisdom/ww4eii.htm

"Feather Picking in Pet Birds"
Sam Vaughan DVM
www.vetcity.com/Infocenter/AvianFeatherPicking.html

"Feeding Organic Foods Affordably"
Carolyn Swicegood, *Winged Wisdom*
www.birdsnways.com/wisdom/ww21eii.htm

"Feeding Your Pet Bird"
Petra Burgmann DVM
www.claviaryonline.com/books.html

Gillian's Help Desk
Gillian Willis
www.exoticbird.com/gillian/

"Gram Stain"
Scott McDonald DVM
www.parrottalk.com/gramstain.html

Hagen Tropican Granulated Diets
www.hagen.com/uk/birds/basic/4-4.cfm
www.claviaryonline.com/hagen.html

Harrison's Bird Foods
www.harrisonsbirdfoods.com/
www.claviaryonline.com/hagen.html

"Hazardous Plants"
Birds n Ways
www.birdsnways.com/articles/plntstox.htm

"Holiday & Winter Hazards for Pet Birds"
Carol Highfill, *Winged Wisdom*
www.birdsnways.com/wisdom/ww17e.htm

"How Clean is Clean?"
Developing Your Sanitation Program
www.multiscope.com/hotspot/howcln4.htm

"How Does an Egg Become a Bird?"
www.jobird.com/eggdevel.htm

"How to Manage Feather Picking"
Richard W. Woerpel & Walter J. Rosskopf, Jr.
www.multiscope.com/hotspot/featherpicking.htm

"The Incredible Female Bird Reproductive System"
Linda Pesek DVM
www.birdsnways.com/wisdom/ww32eiv.htm

"Infectious Diseases of Birds"
Santa Clara Pet Hospital
www.santaclarapethospital.com/avdizez.htm

Land of Vos
landofvos.com/

"The Male Bird Reproductive System"
Linda Pesek DVM, *Winged Wisdom*
www.birdsnways.com/wisdom/ww33eiv.htm

"The Marvelous Avian Eye"
Linda Pesek DVM, *Winged Wisdom*
www.wingedwisdom.com/ww31eii.htm

Moonlight Greys
The African Queen's Singing Greys
www.parrottalk.com/art1.htm
www.afqueen.com/

Music Recommendations for African Greys
www.parrottalk.com/amazoncd.html

"The New Bird Exam"
Lisa Paul DVM
www.birdsnways.com/wisdom/ww13eiii.htm

"Nit pickers Physical Exam"
Fern Van Sant DVM
www.funnyfarmexotics.com/IAS/physical.htm

Nutribiotic (GSE)
www.nutribiotic.com/

"Nutrition Expert Panel Review: New Rules for Feeding Pet Birds"
shell.pubnix.net/~mhagen/docu/nutpanel.html

"Nutritional Observations, Hand-Feeding Formulas, and Digestion in Exotic Birds"
shell.pubnix.net/~mhagen/docu/tabcon3.html

The Oasis Sanctuary
www.the-oasis.org/

Old World Aviaries
www.oldworldaviaries.com/

Parrot Care Information Page
Veterinary Associates Stonefield
www.vetcity.com/Infocenter/Parrots.html

"Parrots, Produce & Pesticides"
Carolyn Swicegood, *Winged Wisdom*
www.birdsnways.com/wisdom/ww18eii.htm

Parrot Talk Connection
www.ParrotTalk.com

PBFD Diagnostic Flowchart
IAS 1994
www.funnyfarmexotics.com/IAS/pbfdflow.htm

"Plants Considered Harmful to Birds"
www.netpets.org/birds/healthspa/toxic3.html

"Poisonous Foods, Metals & Compounds"
Birds N Ways
www.birdsnways.com/articles/poisons.htm

"Prevention of Avian Polyomavirus Infections Through Vaccination"
Branson W. Ritchie, DVM, PhD, Kenneth S. Latimer, DVM, PhD, Cheryl B. Greenacre, DVM, Denise Pesti, MS, Raymond Campagnoli, MS, Phil D. Lukert, DVM, PhD
www.funnyfarmexotics.com/IAS/poly98.htm

"Psittacine Pediatrics: Housing and Feeding of Baby Parrots"
Mark Hagen
shell.pubnix.net/~mhagen/docu/tabcon4.html

"Quaker Mutilation Syndrome"
Theresa Jordan, *Winged Wisdom*
www.birdsnways.com/wisdom/ww19eiv.htm

"Questions To Ask The Breeder And/Or Pet Shop"
Sally Blanchard
www.companionparrot.com/articles/questions.html

"Safe Plants and Trees"
Birds n Ways
www.birdsnways.com/articles/plntsafe.htm

"Scented Candles Kill Pet Birds!"
Monica Sudds
www.quakerville.net/qic/q_glade.asp

"Seizures in Pet Birds"
Linda Pesek DVM, Diplomate ABVP (Avian)
Winged Wisdom
www.birdsnways.com/wisdom/ww56eiv.htm

"Selecting a Good Home for Your Baby Birds"
Anne Johnson, *Winged Wisdom*
www.birdsnways.com/wisdom/ww9eiii.htm

"Silent Killer (Teflon, PTFE)"
Joanie Doss
www.parrothouse.com/silentkiller.html

"Sprouting For Healthier Birds"
Carolyn Swicegood, *Winged Wisdom*
www.birdsnways.com/wisdom/ww32e.htm

"The Subject is ALEX"
Kenn Kaufman
www.alexfoundation.org/research/articles/subisalx.
html

"Summer Hazards & Precautions"
Carol Highfill, *Winged Wisdom*
www.birdsnways.com/wisdom/ww13e.htm

USDA Nutrient Data Laboratory
www.nal.usda.gov/fnic/foodcomp/search/

"Using Homeopathics After A Vet Check"
Psychological Feather Picking
www.realmacaw.com/pages/homeo.html

"Ventilation Systems for Indoor Breeding Facilities"
Mark Hagen
shell.pubnix.net/~mhagen/docu/tabcon8.html

Veterinary Support Personnel Network
Avian pages
www.vspn.org/LIBRARY/WWWDirectory/Avian.htm

Winged Wisdom
On-Line Pet Bird Magazine
www.birdsnways.com/wisdom/

ZeiglerFeed
www.zeiglerfeed.com/petzoo.asp
www.claviaryonline.com/hagen.html